TEACHING
IMPROV SKILLS

TEACHING IMPROV SKILLS

Stories, Games, and Tips to Develop Skills
for Improvisational Comedy Troupes

Nancy L. Meyer

TEACHING IMPROV SKILLS
Stories, Games, and Tips to Develop Skills for Improvisational
Comedy Troupes
© Copyright 2022 Nancy L. Meyer
All rights reserved.

Names, characters, places, and incidents either are the product of the author's imagination or are used fictitiously. Any resemblance to actual persons, living or dead, events, or locales is entirely coincidental.

For author interviews, bulk copies, or more information, go to
https://www.nancyproofed.com

Published by Nancy L. Meyer
Diagram Designs: Ashley Williamson Design
Cover designer: Jeanly Zamora
Editor: Margaret A. Harrell

Get Your Free Gift!

Need some help establishing a school improv troupe?

Download

**How to Set Up a School Improv
Troupe: The Logistics**
to take the next steps.

Click <u>here</u> to get your copy.

To Katie and Abby

I am eternally grateful for your dubbing me

"The Funny Mom."

CONTENTS

CONTENTS

FOREWORD

By
Josh D. Ruben, M. Ed.

CONGRATS ON CHOOSING THIS BOOK!

This is it! You did it! You found the book that will improve your life! Your career! Heck, it will even make you look cool at Starbucks! Even now, you look really cool. This book is about Improvisation. It is also about teaching. Most importantly, it is about teaching improvisation and the myriad benefits this provides. Teachers, artists, entrepreneurs, professionals, and even the military all utilize improv in their work.

Thanks to Nancy and some other very important people along the way, I have had a successful performing career, and I'm now lucky to have embarked on a second career in full-time teaching. I teach theatre, direct plays, and teach and perform improv and the occasional play or musical. I'm excited about the lessons in this book for my students and my own growth as an improvisor.

So, what will this book do for you? Improv, in fact all theatre, is a collaborative process. The contents of this tome will assist you and your collaborators (students, fellow troupe members, co-workers, clients, etc.) in building an emotional connection to the task at hand. When we are emotionally connected, we learn better and enjoy the process.

In my experience with theatre, specifically improv comedy, emotional connections are brought about by focusing on two primary components: relevancy and urgency.

Relevancy. Relevancy is at the heart of this book. "Why do I need to know/experience/have this?" Students ask this question every day. Improvisation is relevant in and of itself, but it also teaches how to effectively judge what is relevant and how to avoid or effectively deal with what is not. This is one of the many things about improv, and life, that Nancy taught me.

Urgency. "I need this information/experience/thing NOW!" There is no place for procrastination in an improv scene. Improv, and all acting, is about responding in the moment. Improv proves the adage: "Acting is reacting." Nancy will help you put it into practice.

As a trained improvisational theatre actor, Nancy will save me, you, and the day with insightful, practical, and hilarious writing that embodies the very spirit of what it is to be a professional teaching artist.

Read on. Say "Yes, and . . ." Enjoy!

—Josh D. Ruben, M. Ed.
Drama Director & Fine Arts Dept. Chair,
Northwest Whitfield High School
Teacher of the Year, 2016, Whitfield County Schools, Georgia
2022 Claes Nobel Educator of Distinction,
National Society of High School Scholars

INTRODUCTION

How This Book Works

People might think improvisors get onstage and make stuff up, that it somehow miraculously happens. Sound the buzzer! They could not be more wrong.

Improvisational comedy, whether short or long form or some hybrid, is built on a firm foundation of acting skills, communication skills, collaboration skills, trust, and frameworks. (Short form improv is when performers solicit suggestions from the audience for each three-to-four-minute scene. Long form is when performers gather information and suggestions at the top of the show and use them to perform twenty-five-minute, or longer, scenes.)

Are some people simply born funny? Yes. We can all name one or two folks who fit in that category. One funny person is a stand-up comedian, who writes and rehearses a routine well in advance of a performance. In an improv troupe, the members work as a team to make things up on the spot, spontaneously; it takes good, disciplined work on skills to create funny together.

Building improv troupes from the ground up with middle and high school students is one of my joys. When I get together with others who feel the same way, we share the side-splitting success stories of our kids, relive the laughter, and analyze the heck out of the abilities they deftly demonstrated. It's our way of celebrating the kids and figuring out how to help every troupe member achieve the same outcome.

Since you are reading this book, I gather you, like me, want to help students in or members of your improvisational comedy troupe build their skills. If you are reading it by mistake, keep going. You are bound to be entertained!

Please note that while the exercises and information in this book are targeted toward teachers and students, ANYONE with or in an improv troupe can benefit.

To that end, each chapter has three sections, which follow the same format.

1. STORY FIRST

Each chapter starts with a story of kids and events in school improv troupes or classes around the country. I provide no real names and identify no school location, but they really happened. Each story illustrates a skill that is necessary for producing good, strong improvisational comedy with kids—or adults.

Brains and Stories

Recent research tells us that in reading stories, our brains focus on the characters. Storytelling research reveals that "no matter what form of storytelling the participants used, the brain networks that were activated were . . . affected by the character's intentions, motivations, beliefs, emotions, and actions."[1]

Each chapter's stories build connections from genuine experiences to the improvisational skill. They open a cranial view of how some kids' brains think in or about improv. When you know where students or performers of any age are in their process, you have a starting point for building the skills.

Plus, the stories are funny. At the very least, I hope you'll get a snort laugh out of the tale itself. If you teach drama and/or theatre, you will most likely recognize the type of situations, which will hopefully increase the ha-ha level for you.

Stories and World Domination

In his article "The Science of Storytelling: Why Telling a Story is the Most Powerful Way to Activate our Brains," Leo Widrich discusses how multiple studies by respected brain experts and social scientists show that when we hear or read stories, our brains connect to the characters and relate to their goals. Therefore, when we want people to do something or believe in something or join a quest, it's smart to use stories. Widrich says, "According to Princeton

---

[1] Ye Yuan, Judy Major-Girardin, and Steven Brown. "Storytelling Is Intrinsically Mentalistic: A Functional Magnetic Resonance Imaging Study of Narrative Production across Modalities," *Journal of Cognitive Neuroscience* 30 (9) (2018): 1298, https://doi.org/10.1162/jocn_a_01294.

researcher (Uri) Hasson, storytelling is the only way to plant ideas into other people's minds."[2]

See? World domination through mind control.

2. INFORMATION BREAKDOWN

This section takes different forms in each chapter. It might provide research findings in the area; it might analyze the scene from an improvisor's point of view; or it might provide the thoughts from a teacher's perspective. Pick the information that works for you and/or for your troupe members and students.

3. SKILL BUILDER WORKSHOP GAMES/EXERCISES

After the stories, you will find workshop games or exercises (I use the words interchangeably) designed to build specific skills. As with any art form or sport, some exercises are meant for practice and warm-up. Others for the final product, performance, or game. If you ever directed a school play or musical, you are well aware of how different a rehearsal is from a public performance. Athletic coaches know when certain players are ready to play in the starting lineup and when others might need a bit more practice. With few exceptions, the games explored in these chapters are intended for workshops.

---

[2] Leo Widrich, "The Science of Storytelling: Why Telling a Story Is the Most Powerful Way to Activate Our Brains" (Dec. 5, 2012), https://lifehacker.com/the-science-of-storytelling-why-telling-a-story-is-the-5965703.

Each game includes

- **A Description.** This gives the intention, purpose, or general activity of the exercise.
- **The Level of Play.** While these terms are not scientifically proven levels, I've labeled them as (or a combination of) Beginner, Intermediate, Advanced, or Beginner and Upwards (anybody can play).
- **Grouping.** This shows how many people play the game and whether it requires an audience of observers or if the entire group takes part simultaneously.
- **Preparation Notes (if necessary).**
- **Instructions.** I wrote these in easily accessible language to encourage ANYONE to teach the game.

Each game is followed by

- **Coaching Suggestions.** These will help you guide from the sidelines or make modifications for expansion during rehearsal. Sometimes in extra preparation notes, other times in phrases you can draw on during workshop, I also suggest ways to think about your role.
- **Modifications.** Use this section to simplify the game, make it more challenging, play it another way, etc.
- **Debriefing Questions.** The Debriefing Questions support reflective conversations. The final questions help connect the work to academic and/or social lives, should you choose to go there.

Enough explaining. It's time for a story.

CHAPTER 1

L - A - R - R - Y

STORY FIRST: LARRY

Approximately 1,000 to 1,500 years ago, I taught in a high school that encouraged students to start their own clubs, not unlike other high schools across the universe. To start their clubs, they had to fill out an application and secure a teacher sponsor. With their application approved, they set their time, dates, and locations for their meetings and publicized their clubs. Back in the dark ages, they hung posters and flyers around the school, and since this was a large school, that meant a lot of paper.

It was one of these myriad club start-up flyers that caught my eye. The name stopped me in my tracks: the Hello, Larry Fanclub!

The *Hello, Larry* television show ran one season, 1979 to '80, on NBC. It starred comic actor McLean Stevenson Jr., best known for playing Lt. Colonel Henry Blake on the TV show *M*A*S*H*, and the multi-award-winning Broadway, film, and television actor Joanna Gleason. Stevenson played a divorced dad raising his teenage daughters while hosting a call-in radio show, with Gleason as his smart, funny, caustic producer. Despite the talented cast, the show is widely considered one of the worst ever to reach prime time.

Notice the date. 1979–'80. Yes, that long ago. And yes, people had TV back then. Electricity and running water, too. The bigger point is, there was the poster, hanging on the wall—announcing an upcoming event—years *after* that unlucky season.

Psyched to meet this intrepid kid, I went to the designated room for the first meeting—and I was the only one who showed up. That made the whole thing even funnier to me. This kid went through the entire process to form a club for the sake of a joke. THAT is the essence of comedy RIGHT THERE: intentions, details, and over-the-top welcoming others to be in on the funny.

The experience inspired me. So much so, that I chose the name as my acronym for the skills of improv: L-A-R-R-Y.

L = Listen

A = Accept

R = React

R = Respond

Y = Yes, and . . .

There's a plethora of acronyms these days, and as a former supervisor said, "Some acronyms are more 'sticky' than others." (Thank you, Cheri Sterman, Education Director for Crayola.) The best acronyms are correctly spelled words that reflect whatever the acronym represents. The worst not only don't make up a pronounceable word but go on forever and render themselves useless to most humans. Acronyms should help, not hinder. "L-A-R-R-Y" works for me because of my memory of the phantom club, and it embodies the basic skills every improvisor should cultivate.

I've incorporated **INFORMATION BREAKDOWNs** into the sections about each letter of the acronym.

INFORMATION BREAKDOWN and SKILL BUILDER WORKSHOP GAMES/EXERCISES

L = LISTEN AND THE "IMPROV LISTEN" SIGN

INFORMATION BREAKDOWN

To make the American Sign Language (ASL) word "listen," hold the thumb, pointer, and middle finger up and ring finger and pinky down on one hand. This forms an L. Place the thumb just in front of the ear, with the standing fingers upright, and wave the two standing fingers up and down together a few times. It's a great visual cue, one that has served me well as a coach for improvisors and educators alike.

At a point in my career, I arranged for a sign language interpreter to be present so the students from the nearby School for the Deaf could attend our children's theatre production. As I watched the students with hearing challenges converse together, I noticed that most placed the listening sign on the top of their cheek, just under one of their eyes. When I asked for an explanation, they signed, "Duh. We hear with our eyes. Why put the sign near our ear?" (Yes, there is a sign for "Duh." Admission: Their teacher had to explain it to me. Duh.)

Click! To improvise well, actors must listen carefully to the words and sounds created by all other performers on-stage. In addition, improv actors must be aware of even the most minute actions of fellow performers. Thus, listen with both eyes and ears. This especially impacts openings of scenes and entrances to them, but it must continue throughout the entire performance. To coach my students, I started using this sign, moving it back and forth from under my eye to next to my ear, and dubbed it "Improv Listen."

GAME TITLE: *Alphabet Back and Forth*

DESCRIPTION: Two actors speak each consecutive letter of the alphabet, actively listening for their cue.

LEVEL: Beginner

GROUPING: Whole group in pairs

INSTRUCTIONS:

1. In pairs, designate Person 1 and Person 2. We'll use numbers here so as not to confuse things with the alphabet, which is crucial to the exercise.
2. Two actors stand or sit at the same level, facing each other—their bodies in a neutral, relaxed position; their hands should rest on their laps or by their side. There are no gestures in this game.
3. Using a normal voice and neutral tone, one person says the first letter of the alphabet: A.

When finished, Person 1 simply stops talking, stays still, and prepares to listen to Person 2. There should be no cue that Person 1 has finished speaking other than the end of sound.

4. Person 2 listens to make sure Person 1 has stopped speaking, i.e., all sound has ceased.

5. Person 2 says the next letter of the alphabet: B. When finished, Person 2 simply stops talking, stays still, and prepares to listen to Person 1 speak next. There should be no cue that the speaking is finished other than the end of sound.

6. Person 1 listens to make sure Person 2 has stopped speaking—all sound has ceased—before moving on to saying the next letter.

7. Partners continue until they have completed the alphabet, then repeat the exercise by switching the person who starts first.

8. Repeat as many times as needed.

Coaching Suggestions:

- Encourage students to speak in as neutral a tone as possible. Pay attention to diction and enunciation, but try to speak without any emotion.

- Remind them to face each other. The eyes give us as many clues as the sound does.

- If students are uncomfortable with this, allow them to adjust their positions to make the game work for them.

- Remind them not to cue their partners when done speaking: no head movements, no gestures, no cues of "Go!" or "Your turn."

5

Modifications:
- After completing two rounds using neutral voices, add an emotion to the exercise. The challenge becomes to listen for the sound to end AND to develop a range of speech expression for one emotion.
- Challenge the participants to vary their pace of speaking.
- Try building volume, starting quietly at A and reaching maximum volume at Z.

Debriefing Questions
- What did you think about this exercise before playing? What do you think of it now? Why?
- What was easy about the exercise? Challenging? Why?
- How did waiting for the sound to end affect you? Did it cause you to feel impatient, cause you to relax, or affect you in another way? Explain your answer.
- What did you notice about your own breathing during this game? When did you take a breath? What did you notice about your partner's breathing?
- What happened when you changed emotions (if you did)? Pacing?
- How did this exercise use the Improv Listen sign?
- How will this game help us listen to each other better in improvisation?
- How can you apply this game to everyday life?

A = ACCEPT: TAKE THE OFFER!

INFORMATION BREAKDOWN

Improv is a series of give-and-take: making offers of information, taking it in, and taking it on. Accepting moves the scene forward and builds opportunities for character development, character relationships, objectives, and settings. Let's explain accepting with examples. In a two-person scene, Person A says, "Hey, Grandma, grab the other end of this couch so we can vacuum." Person B has a few things to accept to move this scene forward:

1. Person B is now Grandma and has a grandchild (character and relationship).
2. The aim is to help move the couch by lifting one end each to vacuum.
3. The logical assumption is that they are inside a living space.

If Person B denies all this, saying, for example, "I'm not your grandmother. I'm here for your personal training session," that puts on the brakes and stops the scene. The actor has destroyed any semblance of trust that might have been established with Person A and the entire troupe. That's another topic, but worth mentioning several times. (See Chapter 2.)

Accepting can be challenging for some students, but it is essential to develop with improvisors. Use the term, repeat the term, emphasize the term, and then do it again. Accept and move the scene forward.

7

GAME TITLE: *Yes, Thank You!*

DESCRIPTION: Actors make, accept, and perform offers of simple but ridiculous actions.

LEVEL: Beginner

GROUPING: Pairs within the whole group

PREPARATION: This game can get loud, and some actions can be rambunctious. Set your parameters beforehand and establish a visual cue to monitor the volume.

INSTRUCTIONS:
1. Have partners designate Person A and Person B.
2. Explain that in the first round, Person A will be the "offerer," and Person B will be the "yes, thank you" person. In the second round, they will switch roles.
3. The offerer makes silly offers of actions by completing the phrase, "Would you like to . . ." with actions like disco dance, perform "I'm a Little Teapot," skip around the room, etc. Remind students to keep the offers school appropriate, nonviolent, and nonthreatening. Everyone should feel a level of ridiculousness, but never mortified, bullied, violated, or oppressed.
4. The "yes, thank you" person responds with "Yes, thank you" (or some other positive affirmation), then performs the action. The action stops when the offerer says, "Would you like to stop?" and makes a new offer.

5. After at least four offers, partners switch roles.
6. After at least four second-round offers, freeze the game for the entire group and debrief.

Coaching Suggestions

- Suggest simple, everyday actions, and then build the level of ridiculousness.
- If you notice inappropriate offers or behaviors, intervene according to school/organization policies.
- Remind the offerer to make a new offer every few seconds after the "yes, thank you" person has completed the initial action.

Modifications

- Play the game in trios of A, B, and C. Each person takes a turn offering actions to the other two, thus creating interaction possibilities.
- Play in small groups. Select one offerer to make offers; the group accepts, then immediately does the action.
- Play as a full group.

NOTE: I prefer playing in pairs, as it helps build scene-partner skills while working on accepting.

Debriefing Questions

- What did you notice about the game as we continued each round?
- Which role challenged you the most? Why?
- What did you learn about your own abilities to make and accept offers?
- What did you learn from your partner in this exercise?

- How did you deal with the activity and noise around you?
- How can practicing accepting skills help you in improv?
- What are the pros and cons of accepting skills in everyday life? What will you need to do to discern the difference?

R = REACT

INFORMATION BREAKDOWN

According to good old Merriam-Webster, to react means "to change in response to a stimulus." In theatre, reacting is when our bodies respond instinctively to whatever our partners present to us. The trick is to keep reactions simple and real.

In an improvisation scene, breathing should be our first reaction to what somebody says or does to us. Most of the time, we are unaware of our breathing during a scene, so this exercise helps us focus on how our breath is part of our reactive powers. Before starting, share interpretations of the different breaths we take in different situations:

- A threatening movement or phrase
- Someone laughing with us
- Someone laughing at us
- A surprise
- A person approaching us from a distance with a puppy
- The phrase "Where have you been?" when you are late
- The phrase "I love you" from (a person who might say this)

Movements, we understand: humans are hot-wired for movement, or at least we were before the invention of television. Movements can take many forms: lifting an eyebrow while the rest of the body remains still is a movement; ducking and covering one's head in self-protection is a bigger movement; getting closer to your partner for any reason is locomotive or "traveling" movement.

The trick for improv is to keep reaction movements simple and natural. I challenge students to do the ONE movement they would do in response to any stimulus. Just one thing. But before moving, they must breathe.

GAME TITLE: *Breathe and Move*

DESCRIPTION: Actors concentrate on breathing before reacting with a movement in a simple two-line scene.

LEVEL: Beginner and upwards

GROUPING: Trios within the whole group

INSTRUCTIONS:

1. Place participants in trios; have them choose A, B, and C, and explain how the rounds work. Round one: A = Instigator, B = Reactor, C = Director. Actors rotate the roles in the next two rounds.

2. Observer takes a close audience position to observe the two performers well. Instigator begins with back turned toward Reactor; Reactor faces Instigator's back.

3. Upon the director's cue of "Action," Instigator turns and delivers an opening line, gesture, or

11

action to Reactor. Immediately, Instigator freezes in position.

4. Before saying a word, Reactor takes a breath that matches the delivery, followed by a move that shows how one might react before responding, and freezes.

5. Director calls, "Cut!" Director then describes observations. (See Coaching Suggestions for questions that can support the observations.)

Example:

Instigator: (*Arms on hips, angry look on face.*) Tracy, get down here right now! You have some explaining to do about the mess in the garage.

Reactor: (*Inhales quickly, scrunches eyes, and grabs sides of head with hands.*)

Director: Cut! The Instigator is an angry parent calling to his child who is in another room. The Reactor is the child; the child is in big trouble, knows it, and knows exactly why.

Coaching Suggestions

- Ask Reactor: What kind of breath did you find you needed to react to the Instigator? Why?
- Help Directors describe their observations by using any/all:
  o Describe the move (the gesture, motion, or words) Instigator brought to the scene. What did it tell you about the relationship

between the two characters? How did it communicate relationship to Reactor?

o What emotion/s did Instigator bring to the scene? How do you know?

o What kind of breath did Reactor take? Was it appropriate for what Instigator presented?

o How did Reactor's movement react to what Instigator presented?

o What do you predict Reactor might say or do next? Why?

Modifications

- Make visual cue cards for the Instigator, Reactor, and Director roles (index cards work fine). Players swap cards/roles each round.
- Have partners create a three-line scene based on the exchange (see Chapter 4, Storytelling).

Debriefing Questions

- What did you notice about your own breathing in each round? Your partner's?
- How did focusing on breath and movement help you understand how our bodies react naturally in scene work?
- Which role challenged you most? Why?
- What did you learn from your partners in this exercise?
- How can concentrating on breath and movement help your reactions in improv?
- How can you apply the same ideas to real life?

R = RESPOND: SAY OR DO SOMETHING

INFORMATION BREAKDOWN

Sometimes players need a ready-made* response to which they must add more (see "Yes, and . . ." in the Y section below). After they offer or endow you with information, you have to give 'em something back. You can't leave your partner hanging. When in doubt, say, "Yes, and . . ." (found in next section).

*Not to be confused with Dada artist Marcel Duchamp's Readymade artwork series. Look 'em up.

GAME TITLE: *Remember? Oh, yeah!*

DESCRIPTION: The group tells a story together, cueing each speaker with the line, "Remember?" and starting each response with "Oh, yeah!"

LEVEL: Beginner and upwards

GROUPING: Whole group

INSTRUCTIONS:
1. Gather as a group in a circle. Based on a fictional history of the full group, select the story's theme. For example, it could be "Our Trip to Bermuda Gone Wrong" or "Our Puppy Training Class." The theme must be inclusive.
2. Explain that the group will work together to tell a story based on this theme. Because everyone in the group was in the story and everyone in the group is there at that moment, NOBODY

DIES IN THE STORY. NOBODY. NOT ANYONE. ZERO DEATHS. ZILCH. ZIPPO. NADA. The act of killing off a character destroys possibilities. No discussion of coming back to life or any kind of Frankenstein thing, either. Just no deaths.

3. Determine who will start the story. The starter begins by completing this starter question: "Do you remember the time we all . . . ?" to which the entire group responds, "Oh, yeah!"

4. Briefly, the starter introduces the setting and conflict (after all, the group members are the characters) in one or two sentences. Then the starter turns to the person on the left, saying, "Remember?"

5. The person on the left responds, "Oh, yeah," and adds the next thing that happened, the next plot incident, in one or two sentences.

6. Continue this process, with each speaker cueing the person on their left.

7. The final person ties all the strings together in a ridiculously wonderful, heroic, silly, fabulous ending. Strive for a creative denouement without trivializing it with a third-grade closing such as, "And then I woke up," or "And then I got hit by a truck." Even third graders can do better than that.

Coaching Suggestions

- Encourage everyone to drive the plotline by adding things that *happen*. Help the group understand that listing items or dwelling on descriptions slogs down the story. To make it interesting, keep the action/events going.

15

- Say: In speaking, raise up your group members. Avoid embarrassing, maiming, or otherwise harming them. Also, see the rule about nobody dying. NOBODY.
- If someone gets stuck, offer options, such as "So, we took a walk" to keep the story going, or affirmations of their current feelings that can still move the story forward, such as "And I felt _____."

Modifications

- Upon their entry to the workshop, have members fill a hat/box with story-starter ideas.
- Practice the game with groups of less than ten, then grow the group numbers until the full group creates a story together.
- When the story ends, have each participant write their version of the story told. Share the interpretations and compare the versions.
- Have everyone switch places with each round of play.

Debriefing Questions

- How did you prepare for your addition to the story?
- How did starting your response with "Oh, yeah!" help you add to the story?
- What was it like being limited to one or two sentences? Explain.
- What did you learn from your fellow storytellers in this exercise?

- Which skills did you use? Which skill or skills did you build?
- How did you use other elements of L-A-R-R-Y in this exercise?
- How will this game help us improvise better?
- How might you connect this exercise to something in real life?

Y = YES, AND . . .

INFORMATION BREAKDOWN

"Yes, and . . ." is the heart of all improvisation, no matter the form, topic, theme, group of people—you get the idea. "Yes" indicates the verbal acceptance of the information other partners add to the scene. "And . . ." is the way to bring more to the table and push the scene forward or provide additional information for others to use in the scene.

In a 2006 commencement speech at Knox College in Galesburg, Illinois, Stephen Colbert talked about the intersection of improvisation and life. He hyphenated the two words in the phrase, calling "Yes-and" a verb.

> When I was starting out in Chicago, doing improvisational theatre with Second City and other places, there was really only one rule I was taught about improv. That was, "yes-and." In this case, "yes-and" is a verb. To "yes-and." I yes-and, you yes-and, he, she or it yes-ands. And yes-anding means that when you go onstage to improvise a scene with no script, you have no idea what's going

to happen, maybe with someone you've never met before. To build a scene, you have to accept. To build anything onstage, you have to accept what the other improviser initiates on stage. They say you're doctors—you're doctors. And then, you add to that: We're doctors and we're trapped in an ice cave. That's the "-and." And then hopefully they "yes-and" you back.[3]

He explained, "Saying yes is how things grow." When everybody "Yes-ands," we become open to possibilities and things flow.

GAME TITLE: *"Yes, and" Instructions*

DESCRIPTION: Partners create instructions for a task by adding one line at a time, each successive line beginning with "Yes, and . . ."

LEVEL: Beginner and upwards

GROUPING: Pairs within the whole group

INSTRUCTIONS:
1. In pairs, determine who will start the first set of instructions.
2. Choose a simple, familiar activity for the first round; tell the starters in each pair to begin

---

[3] Vreiss (Valerie Reiss), "Stephen Colbert on the Power of Yes," https://www.beliefnet.com/columnists/freshliving/2009/03/stephen-colbert-on-the-power-of-yes.html.

with the first thing anyone would need to do to complete the task.

3. The partner says, "Yes, and . . ." and adds the next step in the process.

4. The partners continue following the instructions, always starting with "Yes, and . . ."

   Example: Digging a hole.

   ⇒ To dig a hole, get a shovel.

   ⇒ Yes, and carry the shovel over to where you want to dig the hole.

   ⇒ Yes, and hold the handle of the shovel with two hands.

   ⇒ Yes, and use one foot to push the blade of the shovel into the dirt.

   ⇒ Etc.

5. Freeze the first round, debrief, and have the partners swap who starts for a second round. This time, give an unrealistic task, such as "bunny cricket."

   Example:

   ⇒ To play bunny cricket, you will need a bunny, some duct tape, and a flat 3" X 4' board.

   ⇒ Yes, and with the duct tape ready, grasp the bunny by its hindquarters.

   ⇒ Yes, and wrap the bunny into a ball, using the duct tape to hold it neatly in place.

   ⇒ Yes, and make sure the bunny can breathe but not bite.

   ⇒ Yes, and place the bunny ball on the ground, snout up.

   ⇒ Etc.

6. Allow the instructions to continue for at least one minute before debriefing the exercise.

Coaching Suggestions

- Remind players to begin each step with "Yes, and . . ."
- Say: Saying "Yes" means you have accepted your partner's information. Accept and continue.
- Encourage linear thinking so each step builds on the former and leads toward successful accomplishments of the task.
- Say: In describing the steps, make them seem possible, as if anyone could do them after hearing the instructions.

Modifications

- Have members upon entry to the workshop fill a hat/box with realistic and unrealistic instruction starter ideas.
- Have members mime each instruction while speaking it.
- Form two lines facing each other. Designate one person from each line to create the "Yes, and" Instructions for an activity.

Debriefing Questions

- How did you figure out what to add next to the instructions? Explain your brain's calculations.
- Which was more challenging, the realistic or unrealistic instructions? Why?
- Describe how it felt being limited to the same opening of "Yes, and" for each step.

- What did you learn from your fellow storytellers in this exercise?
- How did you use other elements of L-A-R-R-Y in this exercise?
- How will this exercise apply to improvisation performance games?
- Stephen Colbert encouraged people to say, "Yes, and," throughout life. How does this phrase connect to real life?

CHAPTER 2

Trust

STORY FIRST: One Voice

A local church invited the high school troupe to perform a short improv set at a benefit program in the church's backyard. No sound, no stage, no frills, but an opportunity for service doing what they loved.

They decided to play "One Voice." Though they had rehearsed this game, it was their first time before an audience. Sharing a chair, Emily and Nick wrapped one arm around each other's neck. Benny sat in the interviewer's chair and, culling from many suggestions, chose expert dog trainers as the topic. He leaned back, crossed his leg, and began.

BENNY: Welcome, everyone, to "Hey! What Do You Do?" the show where we interview people with interesting jobs. Today's guest is an expert in dog training. Please introduce yourself.

EMILY/NICK: (*Speaking simultaneously as if the two people formed one person.*) Hi, Bob, thanks for

having me on the show. My name is Dr. Barnaby Q. Throckmortonsonjin. The third.

BENNY: Dr. Throckmortonsonjin, tell—

EMILY/NICK: Please, call me Barnaby. Or Q.

BENNY: Okay, Barnaby or Q, tell us about the latest trends in dog training.

EMILY/NICK: I'd love to! First, you get a dog. Then you give it a name. Something like Lucky, or Daisy, or Bunsybootsybiddyboomboom.

BENNY: Bunsybootsybiddyboomboom? That seems long for a dog's name.

EMILY/NICK: Yes, it is.

BENNY: (*Pause.*) Great. How about telling us about your unique process for teaching a dog to retrieve?

EMILY/NICK: You get a big stick. Throw it as far as you can. Like a football player far.

BENNY: Is there a special command?

EMILY/NICK: You wave both arms over your head and shout, "Glingydoffoblurbykonkomoto!"

BENNY: Our audience would love to see you demonstrate this technique!

EMILY/NICK: Sure. (*Waving their outside hands over their heads.*) "Gingyblurb—" (*They cough to cover the mistake.*) Sorry. Something in my throat. "Glingydoffoblurbykonkomoto!"

And Scene!

INFORMATION BREAKDOWN

Some might consider this a gimmicky interview game that uses ridiculous language and slow delivery. But here you have two people saying the same syllables simultaneously and an interviewer pushing them to dive deeper into creative depths. There are no cues, no signals, and no flag waving from anyone involved. Just arm waving as required.

But there was trust. Emily and Nick trusted themselves to play one person with one voice coming up with words and responses. They trusted each other to roll between leading and following. When they made a mistake or tripped over a word, they backtracked, saved each other, and pushed the scene forward.

Emily and Nick trusted Benny to feed them questions that would challenge them to come up with creative responses, as well as support their answers. They knew from lots of workshopping that Benny would push them for the "Yes, and." Benny trusted them to answer everything he asked, no matter how tough the question was.

Build ensemble/trust skills

While an improv troupe's goal is not necessarily to train teams of two to play "One Voice," its goal should be to build trust among the members. It's important for students to learn how to trust themselves, their partners, and the process. It takes time, but it's well worth the effort.

Here are two little charts about trusting and not trusting within an improv troupe. I provided blank spots for you to fill in with lessons you have learned about building trust among your troupe members.

Trusting . . .

yourself . . .

means you understand your strengths and weaknesses and you will work on both for the betterment of the troupe.

means you understand you are integral to the improv. You have a role to play, and you are the only one who can do it. And you can do it.

your partners . . .

means you know you will never be left out there alone, high and dry.

means others will work their butts off to make you look spectacular, and it means you will enjoy it and use that power to make them look even better.

means that if the moment sucks, others are there to make it seem like a symphony.

means you will somehow succeed. There will be different increments of success, but when you trust, you win.

the process . . .

builds confidence, growth mindset, and all the skills of improv. The process impacts the performance.

Diagram #1: "Trusting" chart

Not Trusting . . .

yourself . . .

makes you apologetic onstage, or, worse, invisible to your partners and to the audience.

your partners . . .

causes you to stop listening and supporting others, bullying your way through a scene that becomes a monologue. That's stand-up comedy, not improv. Not all stand-up comedians are bullies, but when you stop working with others in improv, that turns your act into a bully pulpit. (Thank you, Teddy Roosevelt.)

the process . . .

means you think you know better than anyone out there. That's hubris, and it destroys relationships, which destroys good improv. Conversely, not trusting the process impacts your ability to take risks.

Diagram #2: "Not Trusting" chart

SKILL-BUILDER WORKSHOP
GAMES/EXERCISES

GAME TITLE: *Truth Spot* (courtesy of Heather DeLude)

DESCRIPTION: One at a time, members step into the middle of the circle and share a personal truth.

LEVEL: Advanced

GROUPING: Whole group

NOTE: Use discretion if trying this game. Be sure students feel comfortable enough to share a truth, and always give them the choice to pass (see Coaching Suggestions).

INSTRUCTIONS:
1. In this game, participants speak a personal truth to the whole group.
2. Form a circle around a "hotspot" in the center.
3. One at a time, players step into the hotspot and complete the prompt the coach calls. Below are sample prompts:
   - Sometimes people say I'm . . .
   - People never say I'm . . .
   - Right now, I feel . . .
   - I am happiest when . . .
   - Someone who makes me feel welcome here is . . .
4. All answers to fill in the blank must come from a personal truth.

5. Players cannot leave the hotspot until another player enters the hotspot and/or taps them out.
   • The hotspot must always stay filled.
   • Sometimes a player may freeze in the hotspot and the prompt will change.
   • Sometimes a player may step into the hotspot multiple times for a prompt.
6. Continue for a set amount of time until every member has had a moment.

Coaching Suggestions

• Say: Start simple and then go deeper.
• Encourage every member to take part, but create a signal for players who choose not to join in to pass. Give students their own voice and choice. However, find private time with the reluctant few to discuss their reasons for not taking part and encourage their eventual participation.
• Additional prompt ideas:
  o If I could, I would . . .
  o I wonder if . . .
  o One day I will . . .
  o A person in this room I admire is . . .
  o The last time I laughed was . . .
  o The last time I cried was . . .
  o I get angry or annoyed when . . .
  o I'm fantastic at . . .
  o I wish I were better at . . .
  o My parents want to think I'm . . .
  o I am insecure about . . .

Modifications

- Have troupe members create the prompts. They can write prompts on small pieces of paper and collect them in a hat or box, or they can submit them electronically beforehand.
- Create new ways for the players to complete each prompt. For experienced troupes, players can freestyle their responses or create an interpretive dance or a pantomime.
- Use this exercise in theater rehearsals for actors to explore the truths of their characters.

Debriefing Questions

1. Before you played it, what did you think about this exercise? What do you think of it now? Why?
2. Why is it important to explore the concepts of truth and trust in improvisation?
3. How does truth build trust?
4. What was easy about the exercise? Challenging? Why?
5. What surprised you about your own answers? Why?
6. What did you learn about your fellow players? How will this help you make choices in improvisational situations?
7. How will this game help us as a group to improvise?
8. How can you apply this game to everyday life?

GAME TITLE: *Story of My Name*

DESCRIPTION: Players share a brief story about their name.

LEVEL: Beginner and upwards

GROUPING: Player circles (five to ten participants in each)

INSTRUCTIONS:
1. Players sit, facing each other in a circle. Appoint a timer and determine the cues to alert each speaker at fifteen seconds and finish time.
2. The first volunteer tells a one-to-two-minute story involving their first name. Some story ideas include
   - The history of their name
   - Why the name was chosen for them
   - The etymology of their name
   - A time when their name was important
   - A time they met someone with the same name
   - A situation where their name served them well
3. After the participant shares the story, one or two people point out something they found interesting in it. They do not ask questions; they show their investment in listening by offering a positive response about something they heard.
4. Everyone in the circle takes turns sharing their name story and receiving comments.

EXAMPLE:

> In one church my husband and I belonged to, there were fourteen women named Nancy. There was even another Nancy Meyer, spelled just like my name (which is unusual because there are many ways to spell Meyer)! I found this out when the minister mailed me a thank-you note for the lovely gift of homemade blackberry preserves. Now, I could have said, "You're welcome," but I hadn't been the cook. So, after I told her I wished I had the skill to make her homemade preserves, we laughed, and she arranged for the other Nancy Meyer and me to meet.
>
> In the first ten minutes, Nancy and I found out we had even more in common than just our names! She had a powerful laugh and a fierce sense of humor, something I proudly wear as well. She married a man with Wisconsin roots—my father-in-law is from Wisconsin. She was a high school art teacher—I was an arts integration specialist who had taught theatre in schools for years. She had two adopted children—I also have two. We both loved reading, movies, and family time, and we became fast friends.

The moral of the story is: Tell the truth about blackberry preserves.

Listening participant #1: The fact that there were fourteen Nancys in the same group is funny!

Listening participant #2: It's interesting that you had more in common than your names.

Coaching Suggestions

- Encourage the speakers to consider what they want to share about their name. Is it something personal or more impersonal? Anecdotal or factual?
- Encourage the speaker to make eye contact with two or more people in the circle.
- Say: Use active listening skills. Look at the speaker. If the speaker looks at you, acknowledge them.
- Remind listeners to find a point of interest from the story. This might be something unusual, a new piece of information, a fascinating detail, etc.

Modifications

- Give participants a choice of telling a story about their first or last name.
- Pair up participants to share their name stories. Change partners several times and share the same story. Have participants think about the ways they changed their story each time. What details did they add? What did they choose to leave out?
- Pair up participants to share their name stories. Afterwards, have them introduce their partners and share one point of interest from the story with the group.

Debriefing Questions
- How is this game about trust?
- How is this game about building ensemble skills?
- What did you learn about someone else? About yourself?
- What L-A-R-R-Y skills are used in this game?
- How will this game help us as a group to improvise?
- How does this game apply to everyday life?

GAME TITLE: *One-Word Story*

DESCRIPTION: Players tell a story, each person adding one word at a time.

LEVEL: Beginner and upwards

GROUPING: Player circles (five to ten participants in each)

INSTRUCTIONS:
1. Have five to ten players stand as they are able in a circle, facing center; select a starter for each circle.
2. Beginning with the starter and moving around the circle in a predetermined direction, the players create a story based on a suggestion, adding one word at a time. Remember, articles such as "the" or "an" count as a word.
3. Go around the circle at least a dozen times.
4. When the story finishes, talk about the plotline as well as how the group kept it building.

Coaching Suggestions

- Remind players to accept all information and encourage a silent, "Yes, and . . ."
- Say: Use correct grammar!
- Say: Let your voice intonation show when a sentence has ended.
- Coach players to move the story forward with action rather than over-describing things (except when necessary to the action).

Modifications

- Repeat the game with a new topic and have group members change places in the circle or mix members to create new circles.
- Have the rest of the group surround the players, fishbowl style, and share observations afterwards.
- Change the number of words each player is allowed to contribute to the story; i.e., have players each add two words. Play another round, with each player adding three or four or five words.
- After a story reaches its denouement, have a member or a player outside the circle retell the story to the group in its entirety.
- Afterwards, create a series of tableaux to retell the story.

Debriefing Questions

- What did you think about this exercise before playing? What do you think of it now? Why?
- What was easy about the exercise? Challenging? Why?

- How often did you need to add articles to the story? How did you feel about it? Explain your answer.
- How is this a game of leading and following? Give-and-take?
- How is this game about trust?
- How is this game about building ensemble skills?
- What are the L-A-R-R-Y skills in this game?
- How will this game help us as a group to improvise?
- How does this game apply to everyday life?

GAME TITLE: *Research Team*

DESCRIPTION: In an interview-style setup, players use all available means to research answers their experts need support on.

LEVEL: Beginner and upwards

GROUPING: Whole group

NOTE: This game prepares beginners to play "Experts." See Chapter 8, "Know Some Stuff."

INSTRUCTIONS:
1. This game takes the format of an interview program with a host and an expert guest. Players use available means to research any answers their experts need support on. You, as the coach, control the onstage action. See the Coaching section for information and ideas.

2. Form four teams:
   a. **The Hosts** ask questions about the topic.
      i. The hosts select one person to represent them. While the representative is onstage, the rest of the team works quietly to create questions the host can ask the experts.
      ii. They can write them down or whisper them to the rep. If you have advanced technology, the host can wear an earpiece and be fed questions through the earpiece.
   b. **The Guest Experts** answer questions about the topic.
      i. The guest experts select a representative, who sits to the side of the Interviewer. While the guest expert representative is onstage, the rest of the team becomes the Research Team.
   c. **The Research Team** finds facts/information to feed the experts about the topic.
      i. The Research Team works quietly to find the exact information the guest expert needs to answer the questions of the Interviewer.
      ii. The Researchers can write or whisper information to the guest expert. If you have advanced technology, the guest expert can wear an earpiece and the research team can feed questions through the earpiece.

    d. The Audience/Question Askers ask questions about the topic.

      i. The Audience/Question Askers listen, as a sympathetic audience should, and then ask questions that will challenge the guest expert to dig deep into knowledge—or research.

3. Select the first host and guest expert and a topic for the show. Outline the rules for audience questions. You can allow the host to select questions, or you, as the director, can select the questions.

4. The host introduces the show and endows the first guest expert with a name and title. When the first guest expert enters, they exchange a little banter. This might include the expert giving some educational background or personal background about first getting interested in the topic.

5. The host then asks a question that requires accurate knowledge about the subject. If the guest expert knows the answer, it should be forthcoming. If not, the guest expert can say, "Let me review my notes/Let me confer with my research team," or something to that effect.

    a. The host cuts to commercial.

    b. The guest expert turns to the research team for information that will help form an answer.

    c. While this is happening, the audience quietly counts to fifteen together. At the end of fifteen seconds, they say, "Commercial break over!"

    d. The host welcomes everyone back, and the guest expert reveals the answer.

    e. If it is correct, the host then turns to the audience to see if anyone has questions for the expert. One raised hand is selected.

    f. That audience member asks a question. The guest expert tries to answer, with the help of the research team if necessary, but if the expert is unsuccessful, the research team repeats the process.

6. Continue for at least three to four questions; then switch roles so others get a turn in the chairs.

Coaching Suggestions

- When selecting a topic, it can be helpful to integrate what students are studying in their other courses to reinforce and support their learning.
- Give each group a few minutes to prepare information and questions. Yes, this is against all rules of improv, but they are about to challenge each other to improvise.
- Be aware of noise levels and create systems for noise control.
- Encourage the host to consult team members for new questions to ask.

Modifications

- Give students a heads-up about the topics you will use in the game the next day.
- Create signs for each group.
- Assign a stage manager to hold "QUIET" or "APPLAUSE" signs.

- Set up a timer for research time.
- Allow up to thirty seconds for research time.
- Have students write their questions instead of raising their hands to be selected. The host or the stage manager can pull them out of a hat.

Debriefing Questions
- What was easy about the exercise? Challenging? Why?
- Which role did you like best (whether or not you played it)?
- How did you feel about being on a team? Did you feel useful? Why or why not? How could you encourage the rep for your group to use the team more?
- How does this game require trust?
- How does this game build trust?
- How will this game help us as a group to improvise?
- How can you apply this game to everyday life?

CHAPTER 3

Embracing Failure

STORY FIRST: Kayla's Funny

Each drama course I taught, from beginner to advanced acting, had a unit on improvisation, both comic and dramatic. It's a very useful tool for actors, but that's a story for another day.

At the end of one improvisation class, Kayla approached me. Now, you should know that this young woman enrolled in an arts class for the first time in high school. She needed an arts credit to graduate, and drama seemed to best fit the bill. A straight-A student, Kayla captained the field hockey team and was one of the most serious humans on the planet. Lovely, smart, kind, and on that day, scared.

"Ms. M, do you have a minute? And before we talk, will you write me a pass to be a few minutes late to my next class?"

"Of course. What's up?"

"I need to tell you something," she said. Her lip trembled, and her feet did that inward knee-bend thing that some people do when they are a wreck.

"What's wrong, Kayla? Are you okay? Do you want to sit down?"

"No, thanks, I'm okay. It's just that . . . you see . . . I'm . . . I'm . . ."

"Yes?"

"I'm not funny."

I took a deep breath and chanted in my head, "Do not laugh. Do not laugh. Do not laugh." Filled with relief that something dire had not happened, I thought: *This is one of the best-delivered comic lines I'd ever heard in my teaching career.* Sincere and 100 percent focused on something trivial—except that for Kayla, it was nothing short of monumental.

She took a deep breath, calmed down, and told me she had signed up for this class to get the art credit AND challenge herself. Now she was terrified of doing improv and falling flat on her face. She had a total fear of failure, something she had never experienced as an A+ student and athletic superstar.

We talked it through, and the next day I paired her with Bert, the funniest person in the classroom, to work with in our improv exercises. Bert proved to be the perfect improv partner. He helped her understand how to support the funny by first understanding the elements of comedy involved. Sometimes he'd stop in the middle of the exercise and ask her, "Do you see what I did there to make it funny?" And they would debrief the moment. It was the antithesis of the saying "If you have to explain the joke, it's no longer funny." The more they talked through the comedy, the better Kayla did. She needed that analysis!

And, more importantly, Kayla got to be funny.

INFORMATION BREAKDOWN

Making friends with and embracing failure is essential for improv.

There is an awful lot in the research universe about the power of failure and how it can build resilience if you have the right mindset. And that is the key: mindset.

In 1966, social researcher Elliot Aronson penned a theory called "The Pratfall Effect." Isn't that the perfect use of a theatrical term? His research revealed that when confident people make mistakes, they become eminently more likable. The rest of us can relate to the person better. When we fail in improv, our teammates LOVE us because it gives them the opportunity to build something wonderful that makes everyone look good.

I like to think this is the basis for Charlie Brown's epiphany in the musical comedy *You're a Good Man, Charlie Brown*, when he picks up a pencil dropped by his crush, the Little Red-Haired Girl. Looking at the pencil, he thrills to find it covered in bite marks. "She chews her pencil. She's human!" he proclaims with an even greater love of her flaws.

If you believe that failure is horrible and the world will end if you trip and fall, then it will. But if you subscribe to the "failure is fatal" philosophy, then you have not watched *Miss Congeniality* on a loop, as we have on sick days in this household. In that film, unglamorous and clumsy FBI agent Grace Hart goes undercover as the drop-dead-gorgeous (if not unconventional) Miss United States contestant from New Jersey, Gracie Lou Freebush. In the televised event, Gracie stumbles and topples to the ground at her pivotal camera-focused moment. Later, in her finalist interview, she makes fun of her fall in a way that builds up her fellow contestants, with whom she has forged surprisingly deep bonds.

"I mean, I know that we secretly wish the other one to trip and fall on her face, but oh, wait a minute, I've already done that!"

Gracie's words illustrate the mindset of embracing failure, recognizing it as an opportunity for growth or forging a relationship.

Improvisors know that at some point, each of us is going to fail. But if we approach failure as an opportunity for creativity, if we trust our mates in the troupe to help us build a spectacular snack out of a lemon, then failure becomes a friend. If we fear slipping and falling flat on our face, if we fear failing a bit each week, we'll never take the risks we need to make great improv. Sometimes you have to play the victim so somebody else gets to be the hero. Befriend failure and turn it around to excitement that you have now built the premise for the scene.

SKILL BUILDER WORKSHOP
GAMES/EXERCISES

Each of these games falls into my category of "Guaranteed Failure—and It's Okay" games. Sure, sometimes you'll win. Yay for you! However, at some point you'll fail, and at the risk of repeating myself: Yay for you! Take a grand bow, step back, listen, learn, and move on. You're alive. You're still in the group. You're growing.

GAME TITLE: *Word Tennis*

DESCRIPTION: Partners mime a singles tennis match—with each racquet swing, saying words that fit in a category.

LEVEL: Beginner

GROUPING: Pairs within the whole group

NOTE: This game comes courtesy of Joseph Riedel, improv comedian extraordinaire and lover of long-form improvisation.

INSTRUCTIONS:
1. Pair up participants and assign spaces. Have partners practice pantomiming hitting a tennis ball back and forth with each other, exploring every kind of stroke: forehand, backhand, underhand, overhead, lob, smash, serve—and everything in between.
2. Pause the practice and move to the next step. Solicit categories from the full group. Categories are groups of items that have something in common, words that help us classify similar things. Some categories children learn quite early include colors, shapes, farm animals, names of candy, etc. More advanced categories might be the list of chemical elements, mathematical formulas, languages of the world, New York Stock Exchange listings, characters in Tolstoy novels, etc. Comic categories expand this list to ideas like things you find on the bottoms of shoes, items in Grandma's house, names of Labrador retrievers.

3. Assign a category and have the pairs continue their tennis game. With each swing of the racquet, they must shout out the name of something that fits into the category.
4. Continue playing until one partner cannot think of anything, repeats a term, or says something that does not fit the category.
5. Wait until each group has stopped; then assign a new category.
6. At any point in the exercise, consider changing partners.

Coaching Suggestions
- Remind partners to play tennis and proclaim that every shot is "in." No player can use the excuse of blanking out on a ball that's out of bounds. This will require paying close attention to the speed and power of their opponent's hit, the imaginary ball's direction, etc. It's not necessary to be an expert, but they sure can pretend to be!
- Encourage players to visualize items in the category. It often helps them come up with a word when it's their turn.
- Remind them to listen to their opponent's words. They need to know if the word fits the category and not repeat any offers.

Modifications:
- Change the game to any one-on-one competition involving a ball or other object: volleyball, table tennis (ping-pong), catch, badminton, egg toss, frisbee, etc.

- Start with two players. Nearby, line up the rest of the participants. The two players play a category. The loser of each game leaves the pair and goes to the end of the line, at which point a new player challenges the winner with a new category.

Debriefing Questions:
- What did you think about this exercise before playing? What do you think of it now? Why?
- What was easy about the exercise? Challenging? Why?
- Did your partner ever use your idea before you said it? What did you do?
- How did this game help you connect your body and brain?
- How is this game designed to help us embrace failure?
- How will this game help us in improvisation?
- How might you apply this game to everyday life?

GAME TITLE: *Name Six*

DESCRIPTION: Participants name six things in various categories supplied by their team.

LEVEL: Beginner and upward

GROUPING: Whole group

PREPARATION: The ideal number of people in each circle is ten. If you have a larger group, create several circles of about ten to twelve. Smaller creates too much pressure; larger does not create enough pressure.

You will need a bean bag or a ball or something else to pass around each circle. I like to use beanbag animals because if you drop them, they don't roll away. And they are cute.

INSTRUCTIONS:
1. Form a circle and place one volunteer in the middle who will be the player. Tag a member of the circle to be the first assigner of categories and determine the direction for the beanbag animal toss.
2. First assigner names a category, and the circle members gently toss the Beanie Baby around the circle. Categories can be simple things like flowers, cookies, greetings, sports you play with a ball, etc.
3. In the time it takes for the players to pass the ball around the circle once, Player must name six items in that category. If Player **fails**, Player joins the circle and selects a new Player to go into the middle. If Player **succeeds**, Player stays in the middle.
4. The person to the left of the first assigner names a new category.
5. Continue until everyone in the circle has been Player.

Coaching Suggestions
- The categories should not be so specific that nobody will *ever* win (e.g., children's book authors of the 1940s), nor should the categories be so wide open that winning is like breathing (animals).

- If they are stuck, some suggested categories might be
  o Fast-food chains
  o Recipes for leftover chicken
  o Disney characters
  o Types of reptiles
  o Two-syllable dog names

Modifications
- Create more challenging but not insurmountable categories. These might include classical music composers, 1960s television shows, fish phylum, etc.
- Celebrate each failure with applause or with a cheer.
- Try not watching the ball or beanbag animal go around the circle.
- Instead of passing an item, have the circle quietly sing a short children's song like "Twinkle, Twinkle, Little Star."
- As they improve, play music such as Khachaturian's "Saber Dance" to add an element of speed to the game.

Debriefing Questions
- What was the biggest challenge to this game? Why?
- What role did you prefer playing: a circle member, the category assigner, or player? Why?
- What skills does this game build?
- How is this game designed to help us embrace failure?
- How will this game help us in improvisation?
- How might you apply this game to everyday life?

GAME TITLE: *Questions*

DESCRIPTION: Partners carry on a dialogue constructed of questions ONLY.

LEVEL: Beginner and upward

GROUPING: Pairs within the whole group

NOTE: Can use as a performance game

INSTRUCTIONS:
1. This game challenges the improv rule "Never lead with a question." Remember: rules were made to be broken.
2. Designate Person A and Person B in each pair. Person A will start the first round, and Person B will start the second; continue alternating starters for each round.
3. Explain that the goal of this game is to create a dialogue constructed of questions. Each question relates to (and might even answer) the previous question, builds the story, and adds information.
4. Person A steps up to and asks a detailed question of Person B. Person B responds with a question relating to the first asked, to which Person A responds with a question. Continue until one partner cannot continue the scene with a story-building question.
5. At some point, one of the players won't be able to think of a question response. That's when both players call, "Freeze!" or "Stop!" or "(insert cue word or sound effect)." They step away from each

other and silently count to five (or some other predetermined number) before Person B starts a new question scene.

Example:

Person A: Dad/Mom, would you please help me change my tire?

Person B: What happened, honey?

Person A: Do you promise not to get angry?

Person B: What could you do that would ever make me angry?

Person A: If I tell you I was street racing, will you still love me?

Person B: How many times have I warned you that street racing isn't safe?

Person A: How will I ever land a role in *Fast and Furious 92* if I don't practice?

Person B: Who showed you those films?

Person A: Um . . .Dad?

Person A's answer is a scene stopper because it doesn't move the scene forward or offer Person B any information to build the next question.

6. Repeat the process.

Coaching Suggestions

- Before playing the game, help participants understand that a story-building question gives information and details to build plotline or solve a problem.

- Teach them how to use a statement to create a question. In the example above, Person A's question about landing a role in the famous movie sequel of a sequel of ninety other sequels takes the statement, "I need to practice so I can land a role in . . ." and rearranges the words to form a question.

- Encourage participants to use the CROW acronym (character, relationships, objective, where) when crafting their questions in the scene.

- Help participants think of ways to endow their partners with characters, qualities, and challenges with each question.

Modifications

- Give suggestions (themes or characters or locations or problems or other ideas) for each round's question scenes. Some ideas might include
  - o Parent/child and child missed curfew
  - o Two pirates stranded on a desert island
  - o Sports teammates talking strategy
  - o Friends discussing school schedules
  - o Alien asking a human questions about life on earth
  - o Disgruntled customer and clerk at hotel/café/restaurant/shoe store/amusement park

- Encourage partners to add physicality to the scene; have them DO what they are talking about.
- Play as a full group. Form a large circle and designate the center as the playing space. Two "voluntolds" step into the circle to begin a question scene. When one player fails to continue the scene with a question, the player steps back into the circle, and a new volunteer enters with a new situation.

Debriefing Questions
- What was the biggest challenge to this game? Why?
- What strategies did you use to help you devise your response questions?
- How did listening help you in this game?
- What skills does this game build?
- How is this game designed to help us embrace failure?
- How will this game help us in improvisation?
- How might you apply this game to everyday life?

GAME TITLE: *Story, Story, Die*

DESCRIPTION: Five actors tell a story, as directed by a controller. If they break a rule, they stage a ridiculous, over-the-top death.

LEVEL: Beginner and upward

GROUPING: Whole group, performers, and audience

NOTE: Can use as a performance game

INSTRUCTIONS:

1. Seat the full group in audience position. Select a group of five storytellers to stand shoulder to shoulder, facing the audience. Select and seat one conductor (or play the conductor yourself) in front of the audience, facing the five storytellers. The conductor's back faces the audience.
2. Solicit a story theme/title/idea from the audience.
3. The conductor points at one storyteller to begin the story and talk until the conductor points at a different member of the storytelling team. When this happens, Storyteller 1 stops talking, and Storyteller 2 picks up exactly where 1 left off, continuing the same story.
4. The story must pick up immediately. If the storyteller hesitates, repeats a word or phrase, says something grammatically incorrect, or jumps away from the story line, the audience shouts, "Die!" and the offending storyteller stages a solo, Oscar-worthy death scene within five seconds.
5. As soon as the offending storyteller dies, the conductor points at one of the remaining storytellers, who picks up the tale once again.
6. The game ends when one storyteller remains.

Coaching Suggestions

- Coach the storytelling team to employ Improv Listen—paying close attention to the story being told by the speaking player, as well as observing the conductor.

- Encourage storytellers to create dialogue and character voices within their narratives to challenge the other players.
- Remind the conductor to use simple gestures to lead the story.

Modifications

- If players do not die quickly enough, the conductor can challenge the players. For instance, the conductor can point at a different person faster than usual, sweep the pointer down the line, or create new rules for infractions.
- As players die, prearranged substitutes from the audience replace them.
- See instructions for the game "Genre" in Chapter 8, "Know Some Stuff."

Debriefing Questions

- How is this game a fun fail?
- What do you identify as its biggest challenge? Why?
- This game challenges both sides of the brain. The left side is watching the conductor and putting elements of the story in sequence, while the right side of the brain is concocting the next part of the story. How does knowing this help you understand any of the challenges you experienced while playing the game?
- How does understanding the elements of a good story help with this game?
- What skills does this game build?
- How will this game help us in improvisation?
- How might you apply this game to everyday life?

CHAPTER 4

Storytelling

STORY FIRST: Spiders

Because he was also on the football team and practice time overlapped our program, Damien was unavoidably late for a performance.

Our first game of the second set was "Tag Team Monologue." As every good theatre student knows, a monologue is a first-person speech made by a single person. Really. Look it up. A Tag Team Monologue is when several actors take turns to create a first-person speech together. One actor elicits a topic for the story and begins the monologue, continuing until tagged by someone from the line, who picks up the story, even mid-sentence, and so on. (Specific instructions for this game can be found later in the chapter.)

On this night, Sam asked the audience for suggestions of scary things, and from the many options he chose "Spiders." He began, "I was lying in my bed, staring at the ceiling. The clock kept ticking, but I couldn't fall asleep because—"

Natalie tapped out Sam and continued, "I had a lot on my mind: a test the next day, a swim meet on Thursday, asking Julia to the prom. I kept wondering, *Does Julia have a clue how much I like her?*"

Max tagged Natalie, picking up the story: "As I was struggling to come up with a unique way to ask Julia to the prom without looking like a total idiot, I looked up and saw it. A giant spider—"

From out of the audience, Damien leapt on-stage, tapped out Max, turned to the audience, spread his arms wide, and shouted in a voice dripping with horror, "With seven legs!"

People burst out in applause and laughter. The story had gotten nowhere, but that entrance was spectacular!

INFORMATION BREAKDOWN

Every Scene is a Story

In improv, narrative is everything. Period. A narrative is a form of writing or storytelling that tells a story. Narratives can be as short as a joke or as long as a novel, fiction or non-fiction. Movies, television shows, essays, fairy tales, and myths are a few examples of narratives.

So, what makes a good narrative? What do all narratives have in common? Starting in kindergarten, we learn that every good story has the same basic elements.

Elements of a Good Narrative Story
- Characters: the beings who think, see, hear, smell, say, do, and feel things and change. There are two basic types of characters: protagonists

and antagonists. The protagonist is usually the main character, the one the story revolves around and that the audience usually cheers on. Nine times out of ten, the protagonist is a good person with good intentions. The antagonist, aka "the bad guy," usually stands in direct opposition to the protagonist, and we love to boo and hiss at the antagonist.

- Setting: the time(s) and place(s) the story occurs
- Conflict: the problem characters try to solve
- Plotline: the action, what happens, the events
- Climax: when the conflict comes to its highest point of action
- Resolution: the way the conflict resolves and the story ends: where we find the lesson or the moral

Perhaps all a good narrative needs is a beginning, a middle, and an end. We meet the characters, learn about the setting, and the conflict is introduced in the beginning. In the middle, the action happens, and the conflict comes to a pivotal moment. The ending ties up loose ends.

As every teacher knows, each state follows a specific set of English Language Arts (ELA) standards. Standards define the level-appropriate sets of skills and knowledge students are expected to achieve/learn for each curricular area. If working with students, it can be helpful to use the terminology and/or standards from their ELA classes. For the purposes of this book, we will concentrate on the six components/elements listed above.

SKILL BUILDER WORKSHOP
GAMES/EXERCISES

GAME TITLE: *Location*

DESCRIPTION: Actors use pantomimed movements to establish a setting and what events happen in it.

LEVEL: Beginner and upward

GROUPING: Whole group

INSTRUCTIONS:
1. Divide the group in half. One is performing while the other observes. They will take turns playing each role.
2. Brainstorm a list of locations, objects in the locations, and what people do in each.
3. Select a location, such as a beach, library, amusement park, laundromat, skatepark, etc.
4. Actors come up, one at a time, and pantomime people doing whatever it is they do in that location. They use as much space as they need and change their action as a person would in this situation. If they are in a library, they might search the stacks for a while, then sit in a chair to read.
5. As each actor joins the location, tell the new actor to look at the reality the previous actors established. Where did the reader in the chair establish the exact position of the book stacks? Where is the front door? Where is the checkout desk located?

6. When everyone has joined the scenario, go around the group and tap individuals. Upon your tap, they must freeze in place.

7. While frozen, they augment their pose. If walking, they should freeze in a big stride. If they are reading, they freeze holding the book out with extended arms.

8. Debrief with the observers while the location actors remain in place.

9. Have the actors sit and observe while the second group repeats the process in a different location.

Coaching Suggestions:

- Remind participants to observe before going on-stage! Notice what others have already established and where the stationary things are in the scene.

- Encourage participants to join another person in an activity, especially if it will help clarify details.

Modifications:

- Half the group becomes objects, and the other half becomes the people in the location. Then switch roles.

- Allow actors to add sound effects to their actions when appropriate.

- Once all actors are in place, allow conversations to begin.

- Add a time of day or a time period to the location.

Debriefing Questions:
- What was the biggest challenge? Why?
- How did you use observation to create the setting? What other strategies did you use?
- In addition to location, what elements of the story did those strategies create? Which ones did they use? What is missing? How do you know?
- What is at least one story from this scene?
- How did L-A-R-RY help you with this game?
- What skills does this game build?
- How is this game designed to construct a story?
- How will this game help us in improvisation?
- How might you apply this game to everyday life?

GAME TITLE: *Chair in the Hall*

DESCRIPTION: This is a problem-solving game where, using no dialogue, one actor creates the story elements.

LEVEL: Beginner and upwards

GROUPING: Whole group, each person taking a turn in front of the audience

PREPARATION: One chair

INSTRUCTIONS:
1. Explain that using the one-chair prop in front of the group, each person will take a turn.
2. Demonstrate by placing a chair to stage left or right, the seat facing you. The person—let's call him Juan—is to imagine that someone jammed this chair into a hallway that goes from right to

left stage. The walls are so close to the sides of the chair that the chair cannot twist or turn.

3. Juan's task is to create a silent story around this setting and problem.
   a. Create a character
   b. Create a reason to get past the chair
   c. Create a manner of getting past the chair
   d. React to getting past the chair
4. No character or the manner of getting past the chair may be repeated. Reasons and reactions may be similar, but never the same.

Coaching Suggestions

- Say: Remember, the setting and conflict are up to you. You can make the chair the focus of the conflict or just another problem to deal with. Each actor must create the character, climax, and resolution to the story.
- Tell the actor to think about who is in the hallway. Then to think about the location of the hallway.
- Say: Why do you need to get past the chair? What is happening? Why is this important?
- Say: How do you react when you get past the chair?
- Remind the actor not to use dialogue, but to keep a narration in their head.

Modifications

- Have observers standing by tell the details of the event right after the actor presents the scene.
- Have audience members tell or write the story and then compare notes with the actor. Use it to inform a second performance.

Debriefing Questions
- What was the biggest challenge? Why?
- Was the chair the conflict or a smaller, secondary problem? How do you know?
- How did L-A-R-R-Y help you with this game?
- How did you create the story elements of character, plotline, climax, and resolution in this game?
- Which element of the story was most important to you? Why? To the story? Why?
- What skills does this game build?
- How will this game help us in improvisation?
- How might you apply this game to everyday life?

GAME TITLE: *You Did That So Well!*

DESCRIPTION: One actor—let's say Barry—pantomimes a simple task while the other—let's say Anna—endows the actor with a back story. The pantomiming actor, Barry, adds one more detail to the story.

LEVEL: Beginner and upward

GROUPING: Pairs within the whole group

INSTRUCTIONS:
1. Partner up and determine who will be Person A and Person B.
2. Select a simple, physical task in which pantomiming it would not induce garbled speech from the audience. Examples: milking a cow, taming a lion, folding laundry, hammering nails, etc.
3. Person A mimes the physical task.

4. Person B enters the space, praises Person A's abilities at the task, and tells a brief story about one time that skill was impressive or came in handy. The story should provide at least two details Person A can work with.

    Example: Person A mimes making a sandwich.

    Person B enters, stays in one place, and says, "You spread that peanut butter with mastery. Nobody cuts a sandwich diagonally as well as you do. When you made those sandwiches last week, people almost didn't want to eat them. Each one was a magnificent work of art."

5. Person A continues the action, graciously accepts the compliment, and adds one more detail to the story to make it complete.

    Example: Person A replies, "Thanks. When that guy framed the sandwich, I was so honored. I hope the shelter can sell it and raise money."

6. Switch roles with a new task and a new story line.

Coaching Suggestions

- Say: Use the elements of story: character, conflict, plot/rising action, climax, and resolution/ denouement.
- Say: Tell a story! This is one time where *showing* is less important.

Modifications

- Expand the scene to five, six, or more lines. Limit the length so the focus stays on the pantomimed action and the storytelling.
- Have participants write a version of the backstory.

Debriefing Questions

- What was the biggest challenge? Why?
- As Person B, how did you use your powers of observation to create the backstory? What other strategies did you use?
- How did L-A-R-R-Y help you with this game?
- How did you use the elements of story in this game? Which ones did you use? Which ones were missing? Why?
- What skills does this game build?
- How is this game designed to construct a story?
- How will this game help us in improvisation?
- How might you apply this game to everyday life?

GAME TITLE: *Three-Line Scene*

DESCRIPTION: In this game, two actors reveal the characters, conflict, and setting of a story/scene within three exchanges of dialogue.

LEVEL: All levels

GROUPING: Pairs within the whole group

Worth Noting: A line of dialogue can be any length, from a single grunt to a fleshed-out, five-minute speech. Strive for balance.

INSTRUCTIONS:

1. In pairs, determine who Person A is and Person B. Person A will start the first three-line scene. Person B will start the second, and so on. Within three lines of dialogue, the two actors establish the characters, the conflict, and the setting of the story/scene. Anything else they jam into those three lines is gravy.

2. One rule is that there are **no questions allowed**. Every spoken line must be a statement. In this way, each actor offers information or endows the other person with a quality, power, or responsibility.

3. Elicit information about the relationship between the two characters in the scene. How do they know each other? What are they doing? Are they both doing the same thing? Do they like each other? What do they want? This will often help solve the problem of establishing the characters, so you can check one item off the elements list.

4. In the performance space, Person A starts doing a simple action. Person B enters and speaks. In this first line of dialogue, B must reveal at least one of the three required story elements: character, conflict, and/or setting.

5. Person A responds, revealing at least one of the required story elements.

6. Person B responds one more time, either adding to or revealing the last element of the story.

7. When they reveal all three elements, freeze the action. Switch roles, get a new relationship, and begin a new story/scene.

8. Debrief.

EXAMPLE #1: A first date

Person A: (*Hands Person B a club and practices putting motion with a miniature golf club.*)

Person B: I love miniature golf! It's perfect for our first date, Jorge!

Person A: Yeah, I asked your friend Margo what you like to do, and she told me you like miniature golf. I took a chance.

Person B: Oh, great. You told Margo. That explains why my friends were in the pro shop when we arrived.

EXAMPLE #2: customer and store employee

Person A: (*Being pulled by a dog on a leash, enters a shop.*)

Person B: Welcome to Puppies, Puppies, Puppies! What a cute puppy you have there. Perhaps I can interest you in training sessions or training treats for your fur baby.

Person A: Hi, uh, no, thank you. I would like to return this puppy. It's messy. And it wants to go outside all the time—in the cold! And constantly wants attention. I'm exhausted.

Person B: Yes, well, that's what puppies do.

Coaching Suggestions

- Say: Speak in a way that shows us without telling us!
- Say: Keep your actions simple—one simple movement will focus the energy of the story and give us some information about the character, conflict, or setting.
- Remind players that they are not allowed to ask questions in the scene. Help them think of ways to turn a question into a statement.

Modifications

- Establish a setting or a conflict instead of characters.
- Perform in groups of three. One player rotates in for each new scene; the third becomes an observer.
- Let the scene continue for five, six, or seven lines, but the crucial information must be revealed within the first three lines.
- Write the story of the scene, including what happens after the scene is over.

Debrief the Scene

- What was the biggest challenge? Why?
- What do you think would happen if the story/scene continued? Why?
- How did L-A-R-R-Y help you with this game?
- What were the objectives of each character? How was each expressed?
- What skills does this game build?
- How is this game designed to help us construct a story?

- How will this game help us in improvisation?
- How might you apply this game to everyday life?

GAME TITLE: *Tag Team Monologue*

DESCRIPTION: This is a story told in the first person ("I") by a group of actors.

LEVEL: Beginner and upwards

GROUPING: Five actors in the whole group

INSTRUCTIONS:
1. Line up five actors, shoulder to shoulder, facing a real or imaginary audience. Designate one story starter, who steps forward from the group. Eliciting a suggestion (or taking yours), this person begins the story, telling it in the first person ("I").
2. Other actors take over the story by tapping the speaker on the shoulder. The speaker immediately stops storytelling and moves to the back group.
3. The tapper continues the story from the exact point the previous storyteller stopped. This might be at the end of a sentence or in the middle of a word.
4. People can tap into the story multiple times, but they should be aware of the team. Give each member of the storytelling team at least one opportunity to tell the story before others go for their second or third moments.
5. The story must contain all the story elements.
6. The story continues until you or the actors determine it has finished, preferably after revealing the climax and resolution.

Coaching Suggestions

- Say: Use "Yes, and . . ." to tell the story.
- Remind students to accept and incorporate all information that previous speakers have given. Things can change in the story, but they must not deny the past.
- Encourage students to listen more than tap. Let the speaker get out at least a sentence or a juicy morsel to build on before tapping the speaker out.

Modifications

- As skills build, students will want to tap at a faster rate. This is fine, as long as the story continues to build.
- Encourage storytellers to use the space to tell the story so the next person must travel to tap them out.
- Tell storytellers that if they don't want to be tapped out, they can try to elude the tappers. They must tell the story the entire time they are in escape mode. Be careful about encouraging this, though, and try to keep actors out of the audience space. It's a recipe for an accident.

Debriefing Questions

- What was the biggest challenge? Why?
- How did L-A-R-R-Y help you with this game?
- How did you create the story elements in this game?
- How did you determine when to tap out the storyteller?

- How did you feel when someone tapped you out? What did this inspire you to do?
- Talk about the pressure in this game. How is the pressure created?
- What skills does this game build?
- How did you know when the story was over?
- How will this game help us in improvisation?
- How might you apply this game to everyday life?

CHAPTER 5

Building Characters

STORY FIRST: The Wolf Blitzer Fan Club

For my first few years of teaching, our high school curriculum was for tenth to twelfth grades; ninth graders moved into the building at about my sixth year.

True confession: I initially disliked ninth graders. Silly hormonal babies, they dotted each "i" with a flower or heart. They slapped books out of each other's hands and laughed. When they didn't get their way, they whined. It turned out they needed more supervision than any of us teachers and administrators had imagined. I mean, ninth graders got lost going to the restroom—and not on purpose. The worst thing was, collectively, they had a seriously underdeveloped sense of humor; everything was drama for them.

One day, a girl named Marny redeemed all ninth graders in my eyes. Cue the miracle music.

Marny and a posse of freshman girls registered for my Drama I class. They were doing just fine, performing on target for people who signed up for drama for fear of getting oil pastels on their new shorts, breaking fingernails on an instrument, or looking awkward in a leotard. Maybe they were plain ol' pissed because choir didn't sing pop music. Who knows? I believe they chose drama because they thought their natural skills in nonstop talking made them perfect candidates for every lead role. I worked hard daily to overlook these character traits, but Marny gave me a new perspective in a single moment.

"Mrs. Meyer, do you want to be a part of our Wolf Blitzer Fan Club?"

"Wait—what?"

"Our Wolf Blitzer Fan Club! All you have to do is swear your allegiance to Wolf Blitzer and hang his headshot in your locker—or over your desk or something."

"You mean Wolf Blitzer, the CNN news anchor?"

"Yes, he's so tiny and cute with his little gray beard and his neat suit. And the way he stares right at the camera like he's talking just to you! AH! Doesn't he make you swoon? Here, have a headshot. I've already drawn a heart on it for you. I want to see it up over your desk by class this afternoon!" And she walked—no, skipped—away.

I stood there with my mouth open. This ninth-grade girl had just redeemed the entire freshman class! She played the role of funny fangirl to the Nth degree, committing to the passion for a ridiculous cause, backing up her claim with beautiful logic, and inviting me into her little world. And she had props.

That afternoon I invited her to join our improv troupe. She became a powerful member from day one because she could create ridiculous yet realistic, outrageous yet believable, stunningly flawed yet perfectly constructed characters in scenes of any length.

INFORMATION BREAKDOWN

In improv, building a character depends on the answers to three questions:
- What is the character's goal and/or objective? This is the "want." What does the character want to do? Want to happen? To own? To say?
- What is the relationship between the characters in the scene? They might be relatives, teammates, fellow dog owners, romantic targets, etc. Even being perfect strangers (or imperfect ones) can define a relationship.
- How does the character feel about the other characters?

Actors can express these through use of their bodies, voices, and thought processes.

The best advice I ever received for improvising a character was from a touring branch of the Royal Shakespeare Company. Their advice: *Do something small.*

That's it.

"Do something small" means to start with a small, physical movement: a gesture, a roll of the eyes, or a stance. The infinitesimal movement shows us a bit about the character and what the character is doing at that moment. It's the one thing that will bring you into the NOW. It answers: What are you doing RIGHT NOW?

The games in this section help students "do something small" to define improvised scene characters.

SKILL BUILDER WORKSHOP
GAMES/EXERCISES

GAME TITLE: *This is a Pen*

DESCRIPTION: This game uses a repeated pattern to create character voices.

LEVEL: Beginner and upward

GROUPING: Whole Group

INSTRUCTIONS:
1. Form a circle with the full group and teach the structure of the game, the pattern of spoken lines and movements. Holding a pen, the leader (A) turns to one person on the right or left side (B) and begins the following conversation:
   A. This is a pen. (*A offers pen to B.*)
   B. A what?
   A. A pen.
   B. A what?
   A. A pen.
   B. Oh, a pen. (*B takes the pen.*)
   Person B then begins the pattern with the next person on the opposite side (C), but the pattern expands.
   B. (*Tries to pass pen to C.*) This is a pen.
   C. (*to B*) A what?
   B. (*to A*): A what?
   A. (*to B*) A pen.
   B. (*to C*) A pen.

C. (*to B*) Oh, a pen. (*C takes pen and starts same pattern with D.*) Continue this pattern all the way around the circle until everyone masters the pattern.

2. Introduce the character-voice challenge. Each person develops a voice for their line, which all those involved must imitate. For example, if A whispers, B whispers. When B cries to C, C and A must also cry. When C takes over, C uses an exaggerated lisp, which D and B and A must continue.

3. Play until every person in the circle has created a character voice.

Coaching Suggestions

- Say: Remember, there are six basic voices: high/low, loud/quiet, fast/slow. When in doubt, use one of them.
- Tell them to use emotion/accents/animal sounds/etc. to create a voice.

Modifications

- Add a gesture to each exchange. Everyone repeats the same voice and gesture.
- Add the element of speed. See how quickly they can complete a circle around.

Debriefing Questions

- How many character voices did you hear? See?
- What was the biggest challenge? Why?
- How did you use your voice and body to express the relationship?
- How did L-A-R-R-Y help you with this game?

- What skills does this game build?
- How is this game designed to help us construct characters?
- How will this game help us in improvisation?
- How might you apply this game to everyday life?

GAME TITLE: *Four Chair*

DESCRIPTION: Actors determine how to use setting and/ or situations to play out what their characters want.

LEVEL: Beginner and upwards

GROUPING: Four actors and an audience of observers

PREPARATION: Place four chairs side by side, facing the audience.

INSTRUCTIONS:
1. Explain that you will endow each chair with a place and a want. Whoever sits in that chair will express the want in the given location. Some examples are below:
   a. movie theatre/want to sing along with music
   b. fine French restaurant/want to propose to dinner partner
   c. wrestling match/want to be noticed for enthusiasm
   d. principal's office/want to show you don't care you're in trouble
   e. rowboat/want to catch a fish without tipping over
   f. nail shop/want to relax

2. Have each actor sit in one of the chairs. Have the seated person put the location and want in an "I statement." For example, "I am in a dentist's chair, and I want to tell the dentist about making the debate team."

3. Each person believes that all participants are in the exact situation they themselves are.

4. Actors may react to things other characters say or do, but they may not interact. For example, the person watching the ballet, who wants to show he knows everything about ballet, sits next to someone riding a bucking bronco in a rodeo who wants to hang on for dear life. The rodeo rider might get physical and accidentally bump the ballet fan. Ballet fan may look over with disdain or mutter to himself but may not begin a conversation. The rodeo rider may tell herself to be more careful but may not apologize.

5. Instruct actors they may converse with an invisible scene partner directly in front of them or one at a 45-degree angle away.

6. The first twenty seconds of the exercise must be silent. They should set their location and their want without words. When you give the cue, they may talk. Because they may all talk at once, it has potential to grow loud!

7. Freeze the game, debrief, and replace each actor with someone from the audience/observers. You can change the location/want of each chair or keep it the same. If you keep it the same, encourage the actor to play the character differently than before.

Coaching Suggestions

- Say: Remember to keep the want front and foremost in your mind.
- Ask: Who is directly in front of you? Anybody? How can you include that person in your space? How can that person help or hinder you from getting what you want?
- Coach participants to think the characters on either side are in the same place they are. They may *react* to them, but they may not *interact* with them.

Modifications

- Assign a location only and have participants determine the want.
- Assign a want only and have participants determine the location.
- Change the endowment of the chair to something else that will help them create a character. For example: To each chair, assign an emotion that guides them to determine the want.
- After a minute, call, "Freeze! Move one chair to the left!" Have actors switch to the location and want of the new position. Do this until all four actors have experienced the location and want of each chair.

Debriefing Questions

- Begin with the observers. Ask them to be objective in their statements (i.e., no praise or critiquing of the actors). What did they
  - o See?
  - o Hear?
  - o Otherwise notice?

- Ask actors how they felt when assigned their location and want. Did it feel comfortable? Why or why not?
- What strategies did they use to communicate the location and the want?
- How did the actors use their bodies when the scene was silent to create their character?
- How did they use their voices to create their character?
- Ask the observers what they saw/heard/noticed that reinforces the actor-participants' thoughts behind the character construction.
- How did L-A-R-R-Y help you with this game?
- What skills does this game build?
- How did you use the concept of "do something small"?
- How is this game designed to help construct characters?
- How will this game help us in improvisation?
- How might you apply this game to everyday life?

GAME TITLE: *Hi!*

DESCRIPTION: In this scene, pairs create relationships between two characters who pass and greet each other.

LEVEL: Beginner and upward

GROUPING: Pairs within the whole group

INSTRUCTIONS:

1. In pairs, determine who is Person A and who is Person B. Have the two actors learn their line:

   Person A: Hi.

   Person B: Hi.

2. The characters stand at opposite sides of the performance/workshop space, walk past each other, and speak their line. To create their own character or the action or setting, they may add physicality to the scene, but they must pass the other person. The distance or the proximity is theirs to determine.

3. Have each pair determine the relationship between the two characters before passing each other. See the Coaching Suggestions for ideas.

4. Prepare at least five versions of this scene, each with a distinct set of characters.

5. Perform two of the versions of the scene for others and have the observers describe what they see, doing their best to define the relationship.

Coaching Suggestions

- Use the questions below to guide the group to create their character relationships within the mini story/scenes.
  - o   How do they know each other? Are they friends or foes? Strangers or close friends? Coworkers or boss and employee?
  - o   How do they feel about each other? Is there mutual respect, or does one disdain the other? Are they in love?

o What are they doing? Are they doing something together? Why are they passing each other?

o Where are they? Are they in a courthouse? a school cafeteria? on a sinking ship?

o What levels will they use? Are they crawling, walking, flying, etc.?

o Do they make eye contact? Why or why not?

- How can the actors use facial expressions, tone of voice, movement, and emotion to inform an audience about the relationship?

Modifications

- Allow characters to use a one-word greeting other than "Hi." Think of different greetings, such as hello, hola, hey, yo, evening, etc.

- For more advanced students, do the scene blind. This means not planning the characters beforehand. The actors just walk, reading each other's body language to determine their relationship and how to deliver the line.

Debriefing Questions

- What was the biggest challenge? Why?

- How did you and your partner determine the relationships between the characters?

- How did you use your voice and body to express the relationship?

- How did L-A-R-R-Y help you with this game?

- How did you use the concept of "do something small"?

- What skills does this game build?
- How is this game designed to help us construct characters?
- How will this game help us in improvisation?
- How might you apply this game to everyday life?

GAME TITLE: *The Meeting*

DESCRIPTION: Students take on one of six generic characters to play a scene. Upon your cue, they pass the character to the left and continue the scene in a new role.

LEVEL: Intermediate to Advanced

GROUPING: Whole Group

PREPARATION: On each of six index cards, write one of the following roles: president, nurse, cheerleader, bully, secretary, or derailer. Set up six chairs in a circle facing in.

INSTRUCTIONS:
1. Begin by discussing the role on each of the six cards. Ask volunteers to say the first thing that comes into their mind for each card. ONE THING. Go around the room to encourage participation from every member.
2. Invite six actors to sit in the chairs and assign each a role card.
3. Have the rest of the group form a fishbowl around the actors. Their job is to observe.
4. Ask the group for a generic school-meeting topic. Encourage them to think of a committee to plan a school dance or a service project. The meeting

should not have high emotional or reputational stakes, nor should it be unrealistic or too somber. It should be a generic school event-planning meeting.

5. Explain that the five actors will take part in the meeting according to the character card they hold. Their interpretation of that card is up to them, but they may touch no one in the circle and must not get up from their chair or destroy property—including the card.

6. Encourage them to begin the meeting. When each person in the circle has contributed one thing to the meeting, call, "Freeze."

7. Instruct them to pass their card to the left, read their new card, and continue the scene from where they left off. They are free to interpret the new character as they see fit.

8. Repeat the process until each actor has played at least three roles.

9. Debrief the game.

Coaching Suggestions

- Remind students that characters never "tell," they "show." Don't say, "I'm the president, so we will do it this way," or "I'm the nurse, so I want to make sure everyone feels okay." Instead, use organic language and dialogue the character would use. The president might say, "I'm telling you we need to do it this way," and the nurse might say, "Is everybody comfortable? How do you feel about this decision?"

Modifications

- As the scene progresses, tap a fishbowl member to replace one actor and assume the role on the card.
- Create more "generic" characters for the cards and play with a different group of six.
- Have students create character cards.
- As they become more adept, allow fishbowl members to tap out actor-participants *in front of them* on their own. This establishes limits and safety parameters. Remind them to allow time for the actor to develop the character and/or the scene rather than jumping in on impulse. It should happen at a sensible time in the scene's action.

Debriefing Questions

- Begin with the fishbowl observers. Ask them to be objective in their statements (i.e., no praise or critiquing of the performances/actor-performers). What did they
  - o See?
  - o Hear?
  - o Otherwise notice?
- Ask actor-participants how they felt when assigned their first character. Were they comfortable? Why or why not?
- How did each actor-participant create their character? How did they use their voices and/or bodies to do so? How did their dialogue communicate the role?
- How did it feel to change character? What did you do to embody the new role? Did you continue to

do the same things the person did before you? Did you interpret the character differently?

- Ask the fishbowl observers what they saw/heard/ noticed that reinforces the actor-participants' thoughts behind the character construction.
- How did listening help you in this game?
- What skills does this game build?
- How did you use the concept of "do something small"?
- How is this game designed to help us construct characters?
- How will this game help us in improvisation?
- How might you apply this game to everyday life?

CHAPTER 6

Limitations

STORY FIRST: A to Z

We set up Mateo and Claire for a game of A to Z, based on the alphabet, where each actor's line of dialogue starts with a word beginning with the next letter of the alphabet (instructions below). The setting was a pizza joint, and Mateo was training Claire to make pizza.

The two of them had zipped through most of the alphabet, all the while tossing pizza in the air and, occasionally, onto the floor. After all, comedy comes in dropping things. We pick up the story at letter T. (See what I did there?)

MATEO: Tomato sauce goes on next, but use a light hand. (*Yelling.*) That's too much! We don't make soggy pizza here!

CLAIRE: Use a kinder voice, please. Your yelling makes me nervous. I can't create when I'm nervous.

MATEO: Very well, I'll try to use a kinder voice, but you have to follow my instructions to the T. Our pizzas must meet Pilgrim Pizza's high standards!

CLAIRE: Whoa! You think Pilgrim Pizza has high standards? Are you kidding me?!

> BIG PAUSE. The letter X stopped Mateo in his tracks. As his brain struggled to find a word beginning with X, we all watched; steam poured out of his ears. After about three seconds, which can feel like a lifetime on-stage, Mateo erupted.

MATEO: Xerxes, god of thunder! Give me the patience to deal with this one!

CLAIRE: You think it's okay to call on the gods? And you choose Xerxes? Of all the gods, that's the one you pick? High standards for pizza, but not for the gods you call on.

MATEO: Zeus! I call on Zeus, okay? Are you happy now? Let's just finish this pizza and get it in the oven before I invoke all the gods!

And scene!

INFORMATION BREAKDOWN

Alphabet games fall in the category of "Limitation Games." Limitation games are highly structured; they constrict the performer to a very specific range of choices. Structure is the very foundation of improvisation, and limitation games take it to a higher level.

Limitation and comedy build on familiarity and common experiences—with a twist. The audience must have some knowledge about or relationship with the characters or the topic or the conflict presented on-stage. Most people over six years of age are familiar with the alphabet, so there is common ground right there. The twist comes with never knowing what word the performer will come up with that starts with the next letter. Especially when getting to X. As a matter of fact, almost always when they get to X.

Many limitation games make for excellent workshops *and* performances, and the more you practice them, the better prepared the students will be to perform them. But other than invoking Xerxes, god of thunder, multiple times yourself, push them to create something new each time they play. You might experience a lot of X-rays and folks pointing to where X marks the spot, but keep pushing, and someday someone will use "xenophobia."

SKILL BUILDER WORKSHOP GAMES/EXERCISES

GAME TITLE: *A to Z*

DESCRIPTION: Actors participate in a conversation structured by each consecutive letter of the alphabet.

LEVEL: Beginner and upwards

GROUPING: Pairs within the whole group

INSTRUCTIONS:
1. Pair students and determine who will be Person A and who will be Person B. Have them face each other, sitting or standing as they are able.

2. Assign or elicit a suggestion for a two-person scene, e.g., studying for a grueling test, putting together a puzzle, building a model, etc.

3. Person A starts off with a word that begins with the letter A. This can be one word alone or the first word in a sentence of any length. It could even be the first word of an entire monologue; length is not important, but the first spoken word's letter is key.

4. Person B responds, starting with the letter B. Again, this can be one word or the first word in a sentence of any length. It could even be the first word of an entire monologue because length is not important, just the first letter of the first word. Person A responds with a word that starts with C. Person B responds with a word that starts with D, and so on through the alphabet.

Coaching Suggestions

- Encourage students to listen to all the information being offered in each speech, even if it's only one word. The conversation must appear to be genuine: two people listening and responding to each offer.

- Say: Use your working memory! How can you twist the words in a sentence around so you can start your sentence with the next letter in the alphabet, even if it is unusual?

Modifications

- Turn the conversation into a scene with a setting and characters who have relationships and objectives.

- Start in the middle of the alphabet and return to that letter by the end of the scene.
- For advanced students, run the alphabet backwards from Z to A.

Debriefing Questions
- What was the biggest challenge to this game? Why?
- What line are you most proud of? Why?
- How did you deal with the limitations of this game?
- What strategies did you use to help you determine your starting word?
- Does it seem like you had a genuine conversation? Why or why not?
- How did listening help you in this game?
- What skills does this game build?
- How will this game help us in improvisation?
- How might you apply this game to everyday life?

GAME TITLE: *1, 3, 5*

DESCRIPTION: Three actors (Persons 1, 3, 5) perform a scene where the first is limited to single-word sentences, the second must speak in three-word sentences, and the third must speak in five-word sentences.

LEVEL: Intermediate to Advanced

GROUPING: Trios/quartets within the whole group

INSTRUCTIONS:
1. Three actors perform a scene where Person 1 is limited to only one word each time, Person 3 must use three words each time, and Person 5

must use five words each time in speaking. These must be grammatically correct sentences that contain complete thoughts.

2. Form teams of three and determine who will be Person 1, Person 3, and Person 5.

3. Explain that the scene must seem like a genuine conversation, and each line must respond to a line spoken before.

4. They should work hard at creating complete, grammatically correct thoughts while staying within their limitations.

5. The actors do not need to speak in order, but they must stick to their limitation.

6. Keep the movement simple so they can concentrate on the limitations of speech.

7. Let scenes go for 1 ½ to 2 minutes, then call, "Freeze!" and debrief.

Coaching Suggestions

- Say: Make your partners look good and offer them comments that suit their one-, three-, or five-word responses.

- Remind them to strive for complete thoughts within the restrictions.

- Have them use names, when possible, as it helps scene partners know who is being spoken to, just like in regular conversations.

- Push them to respond when prompted.

- Say: Help your Person 1 by cutting Person 1 off!

- Ask: How can you use your emotions to create reasons to make your restricted sentence seem realistic for the situation?

Modifications

- Build the complexity by freezing the scene and having actors switch limitations (i.e., new Person 1, Person 3, Person 5).
- After switching, either continue the scene or offer a new suggestion.
- Toss in a Person 2, Person 4, etc. (Three is ideal for this scene, but it can be an excellent workshop game to have as many as five people in a scene.)
- Add a person to the scene with no limitations, who can steer the scene in many directions.

Debriefing Questions

- What was the biggest challenge? Why?
- What line are you most proud of? Why? Was it yours or someone else's?
- How did you deal with the limitations of this game?
- What strategies did you use to help you determine how to structure your responses?
- Do you feel you had a genuine conversation? Why or why not?
- How do you feel your scene partners helped you? Explain.
- How do you feel your scene partners challenged you? Explain.
- How did listening help you in this game?
- What skills does this game build?
- How will this game help us in improvisation?
- How might you apply this game to everyday life?

GAME TITLE: *One Line Only*

DESCRIPTION: This three-person game limits two players to a single line of dialogue to respond to everything offered to them by either of the other players.

LEVEL: Intermediate to Advanced

GROUPING: Trios within the whole group

PREPARATION: Before they play, give the group slips of paper and ask them to write a single line of appropriate dialogue on each slip. Clarify what "appropriate" means. This can be a famous line from a movie/play/show/commercial or a song lyric or a popular phrase. Be sure to emphasize "appropriate." Also, ask them to write as legibly as possible because if people cannot read the line, the suggestion will be unusable.

INSTRUCTIONS:
1. In teams of three, determine who will be the one-liners and who will be the free-to-speak-as-much-as-they-want-to person, the controller.
2. The one-liner actors draw a slip of paper with a line on it and read it out loud. That is the only thing each of them is permitted to say in the scene.
3. Elicit a suggestion for a scene that involves three people in a limited space but with unlimited movement. Some ideas: sailing on a cruise ship, waiting in a fast-food restaurant line, coaching from the dugout during a baseball game, working out at a fitness club, etc.

4. The controller's job is to keep the scene rolling by setting up the one-liners with opportunities to use their lines, asking them questions to elicit their speech, and justifying the one-liners' lines (making sense of them so that they fit logically into the scene).

5. Run the scene for about 1 ½ minutes, and then have actors switch roles within the trio and draw new lines.

> EXAMPLE: Scene takes place in candy-making shop
>
> O-L1's line: "Drop and give me fifty!"
> O-L2's line: "It's all my fault."
>
> CONTROLLER: Good morning and welcome to your first day at Snodgrass Candies. You'll work together to pull defective candy clusters from the conveyor belt.
>
> OL2: It's all my fault.
>
> CONTROLLER: Oh, so that's why you have been assigned to my shift. You were the one who set the cluster maker incorrectly the other day!
>
> OL1: Drop and give me fifty!
>
> CONTROLLER: Hang on, buddy. We believe in giving people a second chance here.
>
> OL2: It's all my fault.

CONTROLLER: Let it go, kid. You have a new opportunity to make everything right again. I'll turn on the machine, and you'll see the candy slowly roll out.

OL1: Drop and give me fifty!

CONTROLLER: Fifty is quite a sizable amount of candy to start, y'know? How about if we begin with twelve at a time and increase as you get the hang of it?

OL1: Drop and give me fifty!

CONTROLLER: You are pretty sure of yourself there, pal, but okay. Let's get it going faster.

OL1: Drop and give me fifty! Drop and give me fifty!

CONTROLLER: I like your attitude. Good mantra. How do you feel about this speed?

OL2: It's all my fault.

CONTROLLER: Well, your pal here wanted to up the speed, so you need to adjust your attitude and roll with it!

Coaching Suggestions

- For more information on justifying, see the chapter "Justifying the Unexpected."
- Show them how to add variety to the one-liners by changing the punctuation. Demonstrate what happens when they change a statement into a question or a question to a declarative statement.

95

- Ask: How can you change the volume or pace of your line to create more variety and align with the action and tone of the scene?
- Say: Justify the one-liners in as positive fashion as you can because negating the line will stop the scene in its path. Remember "Yes, and . . ."

Modifications
- Give two of the players two lines of dialogue each.
- Explain that the controller may not ask questions.

Debriefing Questions
- What was the biggest challenge to this game? Why?
- What line are you most proud of? Why?
- How did you deal with the limitations of this game?
- If you were a one-liner, how did you add variety to your delivery of your line?
- What strategies did you use to help you determine how to help your one line fit into the conversation/action of the scene?
- If you were a controller, what strategies did you use to justify the lines?
- Do you feel you had a genuine conversation? Why or why not?
- How did listening help you in this game?
- What skills does this game build?
- How will this game help us in improvisation?
- How might you apply this game to everyday life?

GAME TITLE: *Stolen Letters*

DESCRIPTION: Actors are denied the use of a letter of the alphabet and must work around it. They use words that do not include that letter to carry on a grammatically correct conversation in a scene.

LEVEL: Intermediate to Advanced

GROUPING: Pairs within the whole group

INSTRUCTIONS:
1. In pairs, designate Person A and Person B. Ask for a consonant from the English alphabet and announce that that consonant is no longer available to the actors in the scene.
2. Give a scene suggestion for the entire group or for individual pairs.
3. The first time, play the game for conversation only. As their skills improve, include movement to conduct the scene.
4. Let the scene run about 1 ½ minutes before calling, "Freeze!"
5. Try different scenes multiple times with different partners. You can even allow the individuals to carry their stolen-letter identity when moving to a new pairing.

Coaching Suggestions
- Before playing, discuss synonyms and how to use them to compensate for the stolen letter.

- Say: Use your working memory! Think of synonyms that do not use the stolen letter to substitute within your lines.
- Say: Strive for complete thoughts within your restrictions. What other words that do not use that letter will help you say what you want to say? Say: Use names—but avoid using a stolen letter!

Modifications

- Allow any letter to be stolen, consonants and vowels alike.
- Put groups of four together where two are the actors and two are the "synonym support team." They provide words upon scene actors' requests.
- To make it more challenging, assign each actor a different stolen letter.

Debriefing Questions

- What was the biggest challenge to this game? Why?
- What line are you most proud of? Why? Was it yours or your partner's line?
- How did you deal with the limitations of this game?
- What strategies did you use to help you determine how to structure your responses?
- Do you feel you had a genuine conversation? Why or why not?
- How did listening help you in this game?
- How did you use working memory in this game?
- What skills does this game build?
- How will this game help us in improvisation?
- How might you apply this game to everyday life?

GAME TITLE: *Four-Letter Words*

DESCRIPTION: In this game, actors create a scene based on two (appropriate) four-letter words. The goal is to get from the starter word to the closer word by changing a letter in the word to form actual words within the lines of dialogue.

LEVEL: Advanced

GROUPING: Pairs within the whole group

INSTRUCTIONS:
1. Elicit two (appropriate) four-letter words that use completely different letters and write them side by side where everyone can see. The word on the left is the starter; the word on the right is the closer.
2. Elicit a common conversation topic that all participants will base their scene on.
3. Create teams of two and designate Person A and Person B in each. For first-time players, it is good to seat them next to each other as if on a park bench. When learning this game, they should concentrate on the conversation, not the movement.
4. Person A begins and, in the dialogue, uses the starter word.
5. Person B responds to Person A but not until Person A has used the starter word. In responding, Person B must use an *actual* word that changes one letter in the starter word, thus creating word #2.

6. Person A replies, making sure Person B has created and used word #2 in the conversation. Person A uses an actual word that changes one letter in word #2 to create word #3.

7. The scene ends when one actor uses the closer word in lines of dialogue. There is no time limit on this, so prepare for some participants to finish within moments and for others to take much longer!

EXAMPLE: Starter word: *fish*

Closer word: *home*

A: Louie, my grandson and I are going to head to the lake to *fish* this afternoon. Want to come with us?

B: That sounds great, Fern! Let's *fist* bump on that one.

A: Hey, not so *fast.* Gotta keep my hands limber to hold the fishing pole.

B: Sorry about that. Should we race to get there? *Last* one there is a rotten egg!

A: You'll win. I'll probably get *lost* on my way. Better just get a map and meet up.

B: True. I do win *most* racing games. But you win every fishing derby.

A: Remember that time when you had to *host* the fishing derby?

B: I remember falling off the pier into the lake. I got so covered with muck that they had to **hose** me down!

A: Fun times. Tell you what, I'm going to head *home* to pick up the kid and my pole.

Coaching Suggestions

- Say: Take your time. There is no rush in this conversation. A grunt or a sigh is as good as a word before you speak.
- Say: Use your working memory! Keep the word in your head and use your brain to change one letter. Then come up with your response.
- Remind participants they can talk and take part in the conversation while they think of a way to manipulate the word.

Modifications

- Play a version of the game on paper first. Have Person A write a starter word, followed by Person B changing one letter to create a new word, and so on until they reach the closer word.
- As actors speak, have a tracker person write the changed words in order.
- When an actor uses a new word, have that actor signal or make a motion. The actor might stomp a foot or raise a hand when saying the new word.

Debriefing Questions

- What was the biggest challenge to this game? Why?
- What line are you most proud of? Why? Was it yours or your partner's line?

- How did you deal with the limitations of this game?
- How did you use working memory in this game?
- What strategies did you use to help you determine how to structure your responses?
- Do you feel you had a genuine conversation? Why or why not?
- How did listening help you in this game?
- What skills does this game build?
- How will this game help us in improvisation?
- How might you apply this game to everyday life?

ADDITIONAL GAMES in other chapters:

- ***Partner alphabet*** (SEE L = Listen in Chapter 1, L-A-R-R-Y)

CHAPTER 7

Justifying The Unexpected

STORY FIRST, #1: Unexpected Underwear

Most people don't expect beautiful people to be funny, or at least when it happens, it surprises and delights them. Thank goodness, in film and television, lots of beautiful specimens of humans are proving they can be funny. I could provide a list, but who wants to be responsible for the legalities of that? In general, people are quite often surprised. A beautiful young woman doing PHYSICAL comedy? The shock meter dings before the laugh track hits high.

Amanda could have been a model for all things beautiful, preppy, and wholesome. Suitors fell at her feet, her social skills were unparalleled, and her smile lit up the neighborhood. Still does. Gorgeous, smart—and funny. Even today.

We were at an improv troupe meeting, playing "Guaranteed Ovation."

In this game, one person stands in front of the audience (the group). The individual's job is to make a simple gesture, such as waving. Upon seeing this gesture, the audience applauds commensurately: a polite yet unenthusiastic few claps—or a golf clap (that intentionally quiet applause to avoid interrupting the concentration during a swing or putt). The individual, bolstered by the applause, though tepid, repeats the gesture, only bigger, enthusiastically. Clapping with increased volume and length of time, the audience shows appreciation. The individual then repeats the gesture a third time—in the biggest, most over-the-top manner, bursting with emotion and as much physicality as fits the gesture. Audience members reward this performance with a standing ovation (more on this later). Then it's the next person's turn to do a new gesture, and so on.

The usual first responders got up and performed some pretty typical gestures: pratfalls, bows, preening hair flips, muscle flexes.

Then Amanda got up. Absolutely still, she stood there, smiling at the house, then reached behind her and tugged on her underwear. The group almost lost it, as if it were the ultimate gesture of the game, because it was such a surprise. But it got better. After the first round of applause, she gave a bigger panty tug. The audience went nuts. The third time, it was as if she were wearing the tightest thong ever and struggled to get that underwear out of her crack! The house went WILD, cheering and falling on the floor in tears of laughter.

Curtsying just a little, Amanda returned to her seat deadpan, as if nothing had happened.

INFORMATION BREAKDOWN

This perfectly illustrates "Guaranteed Ovation" because Amanda used a defined, familiar move. Everybody experiences discomfort with clothing at some point. (How people wear thongs eludes me.) The exercise demonstrates a moment of embarrassment—when we do these kinds of moves in real life, we pray nobody catches us in the act. And then it blossoms into the unexpected. Amanda did something nobody would ever assume she'd do, then took full ownership of it. Amanda did this with brilliance.

Doing or saying the unexpected in a solo moment can be entertaining and easy. You don't have to worry about another actor making sense of your choice. However, when something unexpected happens in a scene with two or more people, it requires the art of justification. Justifying is the ultimate "Yes, and." To justify means that actors conjure logical explanations for unexpected choices, moving move the scene forward.

Let's start with a story to explore justification.

STORY FIRST #2: Justifying the Vowel

The scene setup was a version of the TV game show *Wheel of Fortune*. Lenny played the Pat Sajak role of host; Jill assumed the character of an enthusiastic competitor, LaShonda, and Ricki impersonated hostess Vanna White, smiling with sparkling teeth, tilting her hip, and magnificently extending her arm upward near the imaginary phrase board.

When Jill spun the imaginary wheel, Lenny said, "Three hundred dollars. LaShonda, any guesses?"

Jill, now endowed as LaShonda, said, "Yes, Pat. Is there an X?"

Without missing a beat, Lenny/Pat called out something preposterous: "There are three Xs!"

Ricki/Vanna tapped three imaginary panels right next to each other in the middle of the phrase area for the X placements.

Lenny/Pat said, "What would you like to do, LaShonda?"

Jill/LaShonda said, "I'd like to buy a vowel."

Lenny/Pat asked, "What vowel would you like to buy?"

Jill/LaShonda said, "Is there a U?"

Lenny/Pat said to Ricki/Vanna, "Turn over those two Us, Vanna!" Ricki/Vanna placed them at the beginning and the end, the first and last slots, of the imaginary phrase board.

The board stumped Jill/LaShonda. At the buzzer, Lenny/Pat had Ricki/Vanna turn over the letters on the board to "reveal" what words they formed. Without missing a beat, emphasizing the Xs, Lenny/Pat said, "It's that old familiar phrase, 'Upstart Exxxcellence of You.'"

INFORMATION BREAKDOWN

The key to justifying is to accept the unexpected as truth, create a logical explanation, and continue the scene.

Here, Lenny/Pat had to justify the three Xs, Jill/LaShonda's request, and Ricki/Vanna's positioning of the letters.

Jill/LaShonda offered a ridiculous premise; nobody on *Wheel of Fortune* EVER asks for an X right out of the starting gate. It's one of the least-used letters in the alphabet.

Lenny/Pat gave a resounding, "Yes, and," accepting her X and raising her two more.

This is an example of what I like to call a "pile-on." Lenny piled on with his "Yes, and . . ." response. And piled it on higher—to what he thought would be the scene climax—by playing a "Holy Three" card (comedy comes in threes), only to have Ricki place the unexpected cherry on top by juxtaposing all three Xs on the wall, which would presume a word in the English language had three Xs in the center.

Next, Jill piled on by selecting the *least-used vowel* in the English language. Lenny heightened the humor with his "Yes, and . . ." response, and Ricki raised the level another notch by placing each (uncommon) U in an unexpected spot.

Lenny justified each wildly unlikely offer by assuming its reasonableness. He used creative logic, piling on even more ridiculousness in labeling the oddity "that old familiar phrase."

Help troupe members learn how to justify the unexpected, and their improv skills improve.

SKILL BUILDER WORKSHOP GAMES/EXERCISES

GAME: *Air Dancers*

DESCRIPTION: Participants use their bodies to create unique positions and poses until the controller calls, "Freeze!" Selected participants justify their positions as anything except an air dancer, giving information as to who or what they are and what they are doing at that moment.

LEVEL: Beginner and upward

GROUPING: Whole group

PREPARATION: Have different styles of music ready and available to play for the movement portion.

INSTRUCTIONS:
1. Explain that air dancers are those tall, tubular inflatables you see outside stores or big events that flop around as if dancing. If necessary, show a video!
2. Tell participants they are going to stand as they are able and move to music like air dancers until you call, "Freeze!" or stop the music.
3. When you call, "Freeze!" they will freeze in whatever position they are in at that moment and hold the position until you cue them again. If they are standing, their feet must be planted in place. If they are seated, their butts remain in the chair.
4. Tap all but four or five of the frozen air dancers and have them sit and/or drop their pose, becoming observers.
5. Go to each of the remaining air dancers, instructing them they must justify their position by telling who they are and what they are doing, so long as it is anything but an air dancer. For example, someone bent over, with arms extended, pointing down, might say, "I'm a weeping willow waiting for a good wind to scratch my back," or "I'm a lonely jungle gym at the playground." Someone scrunched down—their arms wrapped

around their knees—might say, "I'm a bowling ball waiting on the shelf" or "I'm a kid who did not get picked for a team at recess."

6. When all air dancers have justified their position, tell the entire group to stand as they are able and begin the process again, playing music to help them move. When you call, "Freeze!" tap participants again, keeping a different group of four or five in air dancer position.

7. Repeat the process until all participants have justified their position at least once.

Coaching Suggestions

- Remind participants to remain in place. This is not a locomotor game.
- Encourage them to use a variety of levels (high, medium, and low) in their movement.
- To help them justify, ask questions such as
  - o Who would find themselves in this position?
  - o What would a person be doing in this position?
  - o Would the person be holding or using a prop in this position?
  - o Where would a person in this position be?
  - o Are you a person at all? If not, what are you?
  - o Are you organic or inorganic?

Modifications

- Use very slow music and tell participants they must move in slow motion, concentrating on larger-than-life movements.
- When they justify their position, have participants speak in character as if being interviewed.
- As you go to collect justifications, surprise them with a limitation or a setting. For example, you might introduce the idea that each person is out on the ice on a skating pond or a desert at night. They then must justify their position for that location.
- Once seated, have one or more of the people who were tapped out justify the positions of one or more of the air dancers.
- Add locomotion to the game and allow air dancers to move around the room.

Debriefing Questions

- What was the biggest challenge to this game? Why?
- What strategies did you use to help you justify your position?
- How did L-A-R-R-Y help you with this game?
- What constituted something "unexpected" in this game?
- What skills does this game build?
- How will this game help us in improvisation?
- How might you apply this game to everyday life?

GAME TITLE: *Lines*

DESCRIPTION: Actors blindly select prewritten lines and justify their use of the lines in a scene.

LEVEL: Beginner and upward

GROUPING: Pairs within the whole group

PREPARATION: Have group members write single lines of dialogue on slips of paper and collect them in a hat or basket. Lines can be familiar things people often say, tag lines from commercials, lyrics from songs, famous (or not so famous) lines from movies, television shows, podcasts, etc.

INSTRUCTIONS:
1. In pairs, determine who is Person A and Person B. Not looking at them, they both take two or three lines from the collection and place them in a pocket or hold them—*unread*—in a fist.
2. Collect information to begin a scene and have actors begin the scene with their own ideas, not the lines in their pockets/hands.
3. At any point during the scene, one actor pulls one line out and reads it. An actor, usually the one who read it, justifies the line in the scene.

   NOTE: If the line is illegible, have the actor toss it on the floor and use another from their selected lines or grab a new one from the collection.

4. After speaking the line, toss the paper on the floor.

5. The scene only ends after each actor has used and justified all their lines. The scene should not continue too much past the last usage/justification, but it should come to a logical end.

Coaching Suggestions

- Say: When you've used a line, get rid of it. Don't hang on to it and confuse yourself.
- Say: Even before you know what the line is, think of ways to lead into it. Is it just a part of the conversation, or do you need to set up the line and then justify it after you say it? For example, is this a piece of advice someone gave you at some point? Does the situation remind you of a billboard you saw earlier? Is this an instruction in a manual? Why are you choosing to read it?
- Say: Remember to use logic to fit the line into the scene. There is some reason you said this line. Does it comfort you? Encourage you? Challenge your partner?

Modifications:

- Add a third actor, whose primary job is to justify the lines. (See the game "One Line Only" in Chapter 6, on Limitation skills.)
- Collect fortunes from gum wrappers, tea bags, sugar-substitute packets, fortune cookies, etc. Use them instead of group-generated lines.
- Use textbooks or articles students are reading in other classes. They have to open to a random page and read the first line they see.

- Use comic strips. Copy and cut panels apart and use the first line they read in the panel.

Debriefing Questions:
- What was the biggest challenge to this game? Why?
- What strategies did you use to introduce the line into the scene? How did they work? Will you repeat that strategy or use a different one the next time you play?
- What strategies did you use to justify the line?
- Were any lines in the collection repeats? If so, how did you justify it?
- How did L-A-R-R-Y help you with this game?
- What constituted something "unexpected" in this game?
- What skills does this game build?
- How will this game help us in improvisation?
- How might you apply this game to everyday life?
- What did you learn about yourself?

GAME TITLE: *MacGuyver*

DESCRIPTION: Partners justify using an unexpected prop to solve an unusual problem. Yes, this game is based on the television show and character, *MacGuyver*.

LEVEL: Intermediate and Advanced

GROUPING: Pairs within the whole group

PREPARATION: Each actor should have access to props. These can come from backpacks, the props closet, their own pockets, etc.

INSTRUCTIONS:
1. Partner up and designate Person A and Person B. Have partners turn back-to-back.
2. Each person pulls an item out of his/her pocket, purse, or neighbor's yard.
3. Each person in each pair thinks of a silly problem, such as, "My socks keep falling down," or "There's no more cheese spread at any grocery store!" They each add to that phrase, ". . . and all I have is this [item from pocket, purse, neighbor's yard]."
4. The partners turn around, prop in hand, and present their problem.
5. Partner A says their phrase out loud. For example, "My llama is about to give birth, and all I have is this erasable highlighter!"
6. Partner B says their phrase out loud. For example, "There's no seltzer to be found in the United States, and all I have is this library card!"
7. Partner A justifies a way to use their item to solve Person B's problem. For example, "You can use my erasable highlighter to draw messages and put them in bottles and send them across the ocean so that someone in another country will send you seltzer."
8. Partner B justifies a way to use their item to solve Person A's problem. For example, "You can use my library card to get a book on how to deliver a baby llama safely and everything will be all right!"
9. Turning back-to-back, partners select a different/ unique item. Choose a fresh problem to solve, then repeat the process.

Coaching Suggestions

- Say: Build on the actual use of the item—it is what it is. That's what justifying means. You know what the item is, so find a logical reason to use it in the scene.
- Say: Think of all the uses for the item and how you can expand them. How can you use the item's shape to help solve the problem? How can you use any small part of the item to solve the problem?
- Say: You don't have to demonstrate the use of the item; you have to explain it. This is about using words to justify, not actions to show.

Modifications

- For less experienced improvisors, give them a problem and have them justify how to use each other's prop to solve the problem.
- For more advanced students, time their solutions. Allot pairs 3 minutes total to make their information offers and create their justifications, then cut the time down to 1 ½ minutes, then 1 minute, then 30 seconds.
- Form teams of three and have the third actor play MacGuyver. MacGuyver must solve both problems with the other person's prop.

Debriefing Questions

- What was the biggest challenge? Why?
- What constituted something unexpected in this game?
- What strategies did you use to justify the use of the prop to solve the problem?

- How did L-A-R-R-Y help you with this game?
- What skills does this game build?
- How will this game help us in improvisation?
- How might you apply this game to everyday life?
- What did you learn about yourself?

GAME TITLE: *Silver Lining*

DESCRIPTION: Partners offer each other the opportunity to try ridiculous, outrageously dangerous yet legal activities, finding the silver lining behind each attempt. This builds on the question "Would You Like to . . ." in the "Yes, thank you" game described in Chapter 1: L-A-R-R-Y.

LEVEL: Beginner and upward

GROUPING: Pairs within the whole group

INSTRUCTIONS:
1. In pairs, designate Person A and Person B.
2. Person A begins by asking Person B to try something painful or ridiculous or so dangerous that any human with half a brain would never try it.
3. Responding with unbridled enthusiasm, Person B pantomimes the action, always embodying a sunny disposition, even confronted with the obvious painful consequence of the action.
4. Person A asks Person B, "How was that?"
5. Person B justifies their action by describing the consequence and adds the silver lining: What good came out of the experience? Is it a lesson? A new tattoo? A promotion?

6. They repeat the process, exchanging roles.

   EXAMPLE #1:

   A: Hey, Carlo, would you like to press your hand on this hot waffle iron?

   B: I sure would. (*Pantomimes action.*)

   A: Well, how was that?

   B: It was so hot that I have third-degree burns on my palm, but now I can create some interesting textures when I work with clay.

   EXAMPLE #2:

   B: Babs, there are a ton of killer sharks in the water today. Want to go surfing?

   A: Sounds like fun! (*Pantomimes action.*)

   B: How was that?

   A: I lost my feet, but now I'm shorter than most of the guys I want to date, so a win for me!

Coaching Suggestions

- Before playing the game, brainstorm a list of ridiculous, dangerous yet LEGAL actions others have warned them never to do. Steer them away from anything that would include breaking the law or abusing another person in any way, shape, or form. These should be ridiculous things like walking barefoot in an ice storm.

- Tell participants to keep the outrageous activity small and focused. Concentrate on a single action rather than something that would need more than two steps. Delete "and."
- Remind students to stay joyful/happy/positive in the face of dire circumstances. Everything will be fine.
- Remind them to justify why there is a silver lining. Something good comes out of it.

Modifications

- Build on the ridiculous for one partner two or three times before switching roles. Person A makes the first offer. While Person B does that action, Person A adds another action for Person B to do, which Person B adds on. Person A then adds yet another layer of activity for Person B before asking, "How was that?"
- Play in trios, with one person making offers to the other two, encouraging paired actions.

Debrief

- What was the biggest challenge? Why?
- What constituted something unexpected in this game?
- What strategies did you use to help you think of new activities for your partner?
- How is this game about justifying?
- How did you keep the activity outrageous AND legal?
- How did L-A-R-R-Y help you with this game?
- What skills does this game build?

- How will this game help us in improvisation?
- How might you apply this game to everyday life?

GAME TITLE: *Guaranteed Ovation*

DESCRIPTION: One at a time, participants do a simple gesture, heightening it two more times, commensurate to the increasing audience applause.

Though I introduced this game in Chapter 7 in an anecdote, it's important enough to be laid out in detail below. For consistency's sake, I will use some of the same examples and details from the story.

LEVEL: Beginner and upward

GROUPING: Whole group

PREPARATION: Determine stage space and audience space. Create a "cut" sign for ending the applause/ovations.

INSTRUCTIONS:
1. One person stands in front of the group (the audience). The actor does a simple gesture such as waving.
2. The audience responds with commensurate applause. It's a slight gesture, so perhaps they offer a polite yet unenthusiastic clap or two or a golf clap (*silent clapping*).
3. The individual, bolstered by the applause, heightens the gesture, making it bigger with intensified emotion. If the gesture was a simple

wave with a smile, perhaps they wave with both arms over their head and beam with happiness.

4. The audience shows appreciation with increased volume and length of time in their applause.

5. The individual then repeats the gesture a third time in the biggest, most over-the-top manner, bursting with emotion and as much physicality as is appropriate for the gesture. Their wave might become a full-out leaping up and down, with arms flailing overhead and a joyful countenance.

6. Audience members reward this performance with a standing ovation, full of hoots, hollers, whistles, and foot-stomping.

7. The performer bows, and the next person takes their place to do a gesture.

Coaching Suggestions

- Say: Expand the idea of gestures to body movement. What is a slight movement you can heighten?
- Say: You don't always have to face the audience. Is there something you can do to heighten the movement with your back turned to us?
- Encourage them to try this game with no props, sound effects, words, or noises.

Modifications

- Instead of solo performers, have groups of two, three, or four work together to create a team gesture.
- Play the game with a sound, a single word, or a line from a play.

- Integrate with English Language Arts (ELA): descriptor, comparative, superlative.

Debriefing Questions
- What was the biggest challenge? Why?
- How did you select your gesture/movement?
- How does this game help you understand the concept of heightening?
- Which role did you enjoy more, the performer or the cheering audience?
- How did you keep the activity outrageous AND legal?
- How did L-A-R-R-Y help you with this game?
- What constituted something unexpected?
- What skills does this game build?
- How will this game help us in improvisation?
- How might you apply this game to everyday life?

Additional games in other chapters:

- "Yes, Thank You" (Chapter 1, L-A-R-R-Y)
- "One Line Only" (Chapter 6, Limitations)

CHAPTER 8

Know Some Stuff

STORY FIRST: History Spot

One high school troupe I worked with loved to play "History Spot." Through suggestions and shout-outs, the group collects moments in history: famous historical landmarks, turning points, names and titles of historical figures, etc. A controller uses the list to challenge two actors to present their versions of each suggestion, freezing the actors as each scene hits its peak (or the bottom of the barrel) and shouting a new topic. The actors work from whatever physical position they held in the frozen scene to begin the new scene until frozen again.

The scene prior to the one in this story is unimportant except for the positions of two players, Hans and Caitlyn. Hans froze, lunging on one leg—looking out stage right. Caitlyn froze center stage, kneeling with her arms extended, palms facing in. The controller announced the topic of the Defenestration of Prague. Historical information for clarity: In 1618, a furious Protestant mob hurled three Catholic officials out a sixty-nine-foot-high window; this rather obscure historical moment was a benchmark that helped catalyze the Thirty Years' War. Receiving the skit topic, Hans, the wicked-smart, score-5-on-the-European-History-Advanced-Placement student, exclaimed, "We have to get down the stairs before it's too late!"—exhorting Caitlyn to leave.

Caitlyn, meanwhile, was doing a rapid unscrewing motion with her hands, then placing imaginary items on the ground. Caitlyn said, "Okay, but first help me remove all these fenestrations! We can do it if we work together!"

For one split second, you could see Hans think: *No, Caitlyn, that's not what* "defenestration" *means . . .* An excellent teammate, Hans dropped to his knees and, racing against time, joined her in the removal of those darn fenestrations.

The controller froze the scene and the game as the group dissolved into unbridled laughter. It could go no further than that.

INFORMATION BREAKDOWN

What happened here was the perfect marriage of content knowledge and critical thinking. Hans took his knowledge of AP European History to set up the historical significance of the scene. Caitlyn had absolutely no idea what the Defenestration of Prague was. However, she had linguistic skill. Her brain focused on the prefix "de-" ("to remove") and used grammatical logic to sideswipe the actual history—creating a new (and, might I add, more palatable for comedy) moment, not to mention a new word. When Hans joined her on his knees, he paid the highest compliment to a fellow improvisor—agreement and support to move the scene forward.

The point is, you must know stuff to do improvisational comedy. While European history is a dynamite subject, it's not top of the list for a lot of troupe members or audience members outside of academia. Hans brought academic knowledge to that scene; Caitlyn whittled down the words to create comedy the folks in the house would get. One showed bookish intellectual strength; the other exhibited critical thinking skills and knowledge of grammar to solve the performance problem (and her lack of European history knowledge).

You need to help students figure out what they know and how to show it on-stage while anticipating what the audience knows. The key to good comedy is relatability, and it takes knowing a little about a lot of things to connect with your audience.

So, what is worth knowing to serve improvisation? Everything.

Self-Awareness

Think about what you know and what you know how to do and bring that to every scene. Your audience will detect when you are faking. Look at Caitlyn's performance. She did not have a CLUE what the Defenestration of Prague was and could not fake it. BUT she knew words, so she played to her strength. It worked.

Social Awareness: Friends

Our friends and social circles influence much of what we embrace about our cultural scene. It's how we are wired. Friends influence the music on our phones, the shows we stream, the teams and players we cheer to victory, the hobbies we take up, and clubs we join. Encourage your students to explore information about their own friendship circles and ask fellow troupe members to share experiences. Being aware of their friends' likes and dislikes and their fellow troupe members' lists will aid them in creating interesting characters and dialogue.

There is a caveat in this. Improv allows no "inside" jokes that only a few will understand. It goes back to respecting the audience, honoring their sense of humor. Insider jokes are designed to exclude; comedy is about inclusion. You want laughs? Everyone must be in on the joke.

Social Awareness: Other People in the School and Community

With school-based groups, most of your audiences will come from the families of the performers and kids who attend the school. Therefore, it behooves everyone to know the social structure of the school.

Your students already know the athletes and the artists, the writers and the researchers, the nerds and the know-it-alls in their school—but they need to portray them without passing judgment. Encourage them, also, to notice other groups in the school. Reality is funny enough without imposing an opinion or making recognizable people look bad. Improv is about lifting up your partners on-stage, doing everything in your power to make the others look good. Apply that same attitude toward the groups in your school by avoiding put-downs and embracing the best.

At all times, make sure your troupe members make up names for their characters, especially when reflecting on their peers. It won't work out well if they use the real name of the prom queen or the founder of the motorcycle club. We encourage performers to bring everything they know to the stage, but sharing secrets about others or passing judgment about others is a big red-flag no-no. It's a safety precaution for the performers and the audience members. Remember, you want to build an audience, not alienate it.

Social Awareness: Where They Live

Prepare to be surprised by how much your troupe members know about the community. Then prepare yourself for how much they DO NOT KNOW. We all walk past shops and offices every day, but that doesn't mean we know what happens behind the doors that don't sell snacks and high-tech toys. Presumptuous, yes, but also true. Set up opportunities for those with community knowledge to share with others.

Social Awareness: The Nation and World

When I first moved to Georgia, I joined fellow teachers for a Friday afternoon happy hour. Our barely-eighteen-year-old server asked us for our IDs, and we had a good laugh. Looking at my Connecticut license, he shook his head and confidently proclaimed, "This is fake."

At first, I was flattered, interpreting this remark to mean he thought I was underage. But when he asked for another form of identification that "did not have a fake state on it," all conversation ceased. This young man didn't know Connecticut was a state. Poor boy. A dozen educators proceeded to enlighten him about the original thirteen colonies, the New England states, and geography in general.

Don't let this happen to the members of your troupe. Or friends at happy hour.

Help them make connections to academics, as well as local and national news. Integrate their classroom learning and life learning into workshops and performances. Encourage them to incorporate what they are learning in their core subject areas and their electives. Perhaps the Defenestration of Prague will pop up for you as well.

SKILL-BUILDER WORKSHOP GAMES/EXERCISES

The games listed below require participants to "know some stuff." This might mean scholarly or at least book-learned academic knowledge, or it might be knowledge picked up from living in an area. Debrief the games so students can celebrate what they know and take a moment to determine what they need to know to succeed at improv.

GAME TITLE: *Yes, Your Majesty*

DESCRIPTION: A royal character makes demands on advisors stationed on either side of them. If their responses displease the royal one, they are "dismissed."

LEVEL: Intermediate

GROUPING: Performance team of 6 to 8 and audience

INSTRUCTIONS:
1. Set up three chairs—one in the middle, facing the audience, and one on each side, facing the middle chair.

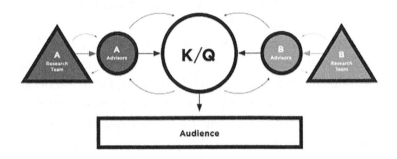

Diagram #3: "Yes, Your Majesty" participant positioning

2. Select three people to start. One person, the king/queen, sits in the center chair. Two advisors sit in the side chairs, one in chair A and one in chair B. The rest of the team members line up on the sides of the A and B chairs.
3. The king/queen alternates between advisors A and B, swiveling in the chair to face the direction of the person being spoken to. With each swivel, the king/queen makes a demand of the advisor to do something or provide information.
4. The two advisors respond to each demand by first saying, "Yes, Your Majesty," and then fulfilling the demand. This continues until the king/queen changes the demand or announces displeasure.

5. The king/queen swivels at will between the two advisors, stopping them in the middle of the demand fulfillment—switching to a new demand. If the advisor displeases the king/queen by, for example, not knowing the newly requested information, hesitating, not stopping their current demand fulfillment, or FOR ANY OTHER REASON, the royal person shouts, "Off with your head!"
6. If the king/queen requests it, the advisor must leave the performance space; a teammate assumes that position, continuing to fulfill the demands of the king/queen. The advisor joins the teammates and cycles in again.
7. If the king/queen stumbles or fumbles or cannot think of a demand, the off-stage teammates shout, "The king/queen is dead! Long live the king/queen!" The king storms off the stage to join the ranks of the audience and taps a successor; the successor assumes the position of king/queen.
8. Continue the game for three to five minutes, then change out characters and repeat.

Coaching Suggestions

-   Encourage students to embody the role. Ask: "How would royalty sit? Speak? What would royalty demand? How would an advisor sit? Speak? Respond?"
-   Say: Make the demands more ridiculous. And remember, keep them appropriate.

- Remind the teammates they may soon be in one of the other positions and turn around is fair play.
- Remind them to use what they know!

Modifications

- Create a royalty team that fills in when the king/queen dies.
- Create a "groundling" group in the audience that replaces all roles as you, the controller, call, "Revolution!"

Debriefing Questions

- What was the biggest challenge? Why?
- Which role was easier/more satisfying to play? Why?
- How did you deal with the limitations of this game?
- As royalty, what strategies did you use to help you determine your demands?
- As advisors, what strategies did you use to fulfill the king/queen's demands?
- How did listening help you in this game?
- How did this game reinforce what you know about certain subjects?
- How did this game provide some insights into what you need to learn?
- What skills does this game build?
- How will this game help us in improvisation?
- How might you apply this game to everyday life?

GAME TITLE: *Experts*

DESCRIPTION: One actor leads an interview; the other plays a subject-matter expert.

LEVEL: Beginner and upwards

GROUPING: Teams of three within the whole group

INSTRUCTIONS:

1. Form teams of three. One person is the interviewer, one the expert, and one the controller.
2. Give teams a topic. The expert KNOWS EVERYTHING about this topic; everything they say about the topic is true.
3. Introducing the expert, the interviewer asks questions about the topic. Some suggested questions include the following:
   a. How long have you been studying (this topic), and how did you get interested in it?
   b. Explain the process of . . .
   c. Explain the history of . . .
   d. How did people first do . . .
   e. How was ___ discovered and by whom?
   f. Why is this important? To whom is this most important?
   g. Show us all how to . . .
   h. Demonstrate how . . .
   i. Teach me the basics of . . .
4. The expert answers each question with the confidence of an absolute expert.

5. The interviewer accepts everything the expert says as absolute truth/fact. It should fascinate and surprise the interviewer or inspire awe.

6. The controller times the scene for about two minutes, then calls, "And cut!" or "And scene!"

7. The controller assumes the role of the interviewer as the interviewer moves to the expert chair, and the expert becomes the controller for a new scene based on a new topic.

8. Continue this process until all three have played each role.

Coaching Suggestions

*   Before playing, brainstorm areas of expertise. Consider combining them. For example, if someone offers "soccer" and another person offers "giraffes," combine them to make "professional giraffe league soccer."

*   Remind all players that everything the expert says is truth. Accept, accept, accept.

*   Encourage the interviewer to ask for a demonstration or a lesson.

*   Encourage the expert to embody someone who knows everything about this subject. If it's gorilla feeding habits, perhaps the expert behaves like a gorilla, occasionally thumping their chest and picking bug-snacks out of the interviewer's hair. If the expertise is in archeology, perhaps the expert constantly wipes off dust.

Modifications

- Have the host hand a random prop to the expert. The expert demonstrates and/or explains how the prop was or is used in that field of expertise.
- Turn the game into a television show with an audience. Create a theme song and have the controller cue the audience to sing it when time is up.
- Use a team of five, so there is constant rotation among the three positions.
- Repeat the same topic, adding a modifier each time. For example, if the topic is "chili cook-off champion," modify it to "air-balloon chili cook-off champion," and then "same-starting-letter-ingredients chili cook-off champion," and then "earthquake chili-cook-off champion," etc.

Debriefing Questions

- What was the biggest challenge? Why?
- Which role was easiest/most satisfying to play? Why?
- As an interviewer, what strategies did you use to help you determine questions to ask?
- As an expert, what strategies did you use to devise your answers?
- As a controller (but not a timer), what did you look for to know it was time to end the scene?
- How did you use physicality to embody each role in this game?
- Talk about the pressure in this game. How is the pressure created? How did each person deal with it?

- How did this game reinforce what you know about certain subjects?
- How did this game provide some insights into what you need to learn?
- What skills does this game build?
- How will this game help us as a group in improvisation?
- How might you apply this game to everyday life?

GAME TITLE: *Props*

DESCRIPTION: Each member of the group uses the same item as something it is not.

LEVEL: Beginner and upward

GROUPING: Whole group

INSTRUCTIONS:
1. In this game, participants use a single prop as something other than what it is supposed to be used for. This focuses on *showing*, not *telling:* demonstrating the item's use rather than explaining it.
2. Select a group of random items and place them in a large container no one can see into. Some ideas include the list below:
    a. Roll of masking tape
    b. Tennis racquet
    c. Baseball bat
    d. Swimming kickboard
    e. Piece of material
    f. Large plastic cup

     g. Spatula

     h. Rubber chicken

     i. Paintbrush

3. Have the group form a circle. Tell them you are going to introduce a prop. Their job is to use it as something it is not. If you bring out an apple, they may not eat it or place it on someone's head and pretend to shoot it off or offer it to someone to bite into and fall asleep until a prince administers love's first kiss. Instead, they might use it as a baseball or a crystal ball or a phone.

4. Rules: Do something physical to show the object's use. Say something someone using it might say. When you are done, pass it to the next person. Going back to the apple-as-phone example, you'd hold it up to your ear, say hello, and chat. It's a nice touch to hang up before handing it off to the next person.

5. The same object goes around the circle, and each person uses it as something different.

6. Anyone who gets stumped can turn to another person and say, "A little help, please?" and people will share ideas.

7. When the object has gone around the entire circle, introduce a second prop and continue the process.

Coaching Suggestions

- Encourage participants to hold the object differently than they would if using it conventionally.

- They don't have to hold the object to use it. Think about observing something they admire.
- Remind them that "show, don't tell," means they avoid verbally identifying their character and the object; they demonstrate/use the object. An example of telling is, "I'm a lion tamer, and this is my whip." An example of showing would be *using* the item as a whip while saying, "Ha! Sit up! I'll show you who's king of the circus jungle!"

Modifications
- Make smaller groups and have them pass the object around the circle multiple times, each time using it as something different.
- Create a scene between two characters using the object as something other than what it is. It can be the focus of the scene or an incidental item.
- Play History Prop. Each player explains the purpose of the item and demonstrates its use during a historical time period (note that this is a "tell first, then show" game).

Debriefing Questions
- How did this game challenge your imagination?
- Which use of the prop impressed you the most? Why?
- What strategies did you use to show rather than tell or vice versa?
- Did you focus on being a character who uses the prop, or did you focus on using the prop as yourself? Explain the difference

- How did this game reinforce what you know about certain subjects?
- How did this game provide some insights into what you need to learn?
- What skills does this game build?
- How will this game help us as a group in improvisation?
- How might you apply this game to everyday life?

GAME TITLE: *Genres*

DESCRIPTION: Five storytellers, each in a different genre, work together to tell a story.

LEVEL: Beginner and upward

GROUPING: Performing team of five with one conductor and audience

INSTRUCTIONS:
1. This game relies on participants knowing about genres in all literary and media forms. They tell a cohesive story that switches genres.
2. Collect a list of literary and media genres. These might include cowboy lit, tween literature, journalistic style, noir, horror, slapstick comedy, nature documentary, etc. Discuss each genre, making clear the qualities or elements necessary to qualify for each.
3. Line up five volunteers, shoulder to shoulder, facing the audience. Select a conductor who sits on a chair or the floor, facing the five volunteers.

4. Assign or allow each volunteer to select a genre and announce it to claim it.

5. The five volunteers will tell the SAME story, as directed by the conductor. The conductor will point at one of the storytelling volunteers. That volunteer tells the story according to their announced genre until the conductor points at another storyteller. That storyteller picks up the story from the exact moment the previous storyteller left off, continuing the tale in their genre.

6. The second storyteller continues until the conductor points to a different storyteller.

7. There should be no delay or repetition, and the story should continue to flow in the new genre.

8. The conductor determines when the story ends. If storytellers cannot end the tale, the conductor points to one storyteller and says, "And the moral of the story is . . ." The storyteller completes the sentence and story.

Coaching Suggestions

- Remind students that the best stories have action, so make sure the story characters DO things to construct a plotline.

- Encourage the storytellers not to get caught up in descriptions unless necessary to the genre and/or plotline.

- Encourage students to listen and not work ahead in the story. It will come together if they know the elements the previous speaker has added.

- Say: Nobody may negate anything already said. As definite lead-ins to their next part of the story, everyone must accept whatever the previous storytellers said. Things can change as the story proceeds, but you may not deny what has already happened.
- Let the conductor have the power to make anyone talk as long or as briefly as the conductor stipulates; the conductor can also create speaking patterns. What would happen if the conductor went back and forth between two storytellers?

Modifications
- Instead of genres, have volunteers use authors.
- Instead of genres or authors, use talk-radio stations or podcast titles.
- Think of other ways to use categories to perform this game.

Debriefing Questions
- How did this game challenge your knowledge of genres?
- What did you discover that you know how to do well?
- What did you discover you still need to learn?
- What strategies did you use to continue the story while bringing it to your genre?
- If you were the conductor, how did you determine when to change the speaker? What clues or cues did you use to make changes?
- How does the element of surprise impact the storytellers and the audience?

- How did this game reinforce what you know about certain subjects?
- What skills does this game build?
- How will this game help us as a group in improvisation?
- How might you apply this game to everyday life?

Additional game from other chapters:
- "Name Six" (See Chapter 3, Embracing Failure)

CHAPTER 9

Physicality in Comedy

STORY FIRST: Gladiators

Elvis and Kamal asked to workshop an exercise called Blind Interview.

Playing the moderator, Mike stood center stage. Elvis exited stage right, and Kamal exited stage left. Both awaited their cues behind a closed door. After canvassing the group for "jobs people don't do anymore," the workshop leader selected "gladiators."

Upon Kamal's entrance, Mike led the group in greeting him with cries of, "Hail, mighty gladiator!" Immediately, Kamal, a first-string football player in real life, swelled his chest, raised his chin, and lifted his massive arms heroically, encouraging the crowd to cheer him on as he strutted on his powerful legs.

Mike asked his name, and Kamal identified himself as Massivus Musculous, a champion gladiator of the Romantic Empire. Interviewed by Mike, Massivus bragged about his gladiator record, greatest conquests, and training regimen.

Kamal built Massivus a background worthy of a Charlton Heston movie like *Ben-Hur* or *The Ten Commandments* or Russell Crowe's *Gladiator*. Mike then asked Massivus to wait offstage. Eliciting wild cheers from his fans up to the moment the door closed, Massivus exited stage left; then he was once again sequestered there, in "the cone of silence."

A volunteer opened the stage right door to admit Elvis, and the crowd shouted, "Hail, mighty gladiator!" Elvis, being a tall string bean of a teen, lacked the physical strut of Massivus Musculous/Kamal. Instead, he drew on his brain power to personify a confident, cocky champion gladiator and, swaggering over to his interviewer, looked with disdain at the crowd, daring them to not cheer.

Mike brought forth the same battery of questions about this new gladiator's name and history. Elvis dubbed himself Brainicus Giganticus, reflecting how his enormous brain power outsmarted and outwitted each opponent. He lacked the sheer muscle of many, but Brainicus bragged how a bit of brawn coupled with high intelligence far outweighed any odds of only muscle with no ability to think of a plan. Helpers escorted him out the stage-right door to set up the next scene.

Note that neither actor knew what character awaited him on the opposite side of the stage.

The doors opened. Massivus and Brainicus stepped inside, and Mike shouted, "Ladies and gentlemen, we are about to witness the ceremonial greeting of champion gladiators!"

Brainicus crossed one arm to the opposite shoulder, then extended the open palm of that hand toward

Massivus. Massivus pounded his chest twice with his fists and pushed the energy toward Brainicus.

Brainicus lunged forward on one leg, pointing toward his opponent; Massivus did two standing leaps, landed in a squat, and roared.

Brainicus took three windmill steps forward, spun around, and rapidly waved his arms out to the side. Massivus took several Fred Flintstone-ballet-tippy-toe steps forward, extended his arms, one over the other, opening and closing them like a Daddy Shark three times.

Brainicus fell to the ground, rolled on his back, lifted his arms and legs into the air, and crisscrossed them repeatedly. Massivus cartwheeled until he was over Brainicus and wiggled his fingers in Brainicus's face.

Mike, laughing almost as uncontrollably as the group, called, "Scene!" and the two actors broke their stony-faced visages and collapsed laughing next to each other.

INFORMATION BREAKDOWN

This game is usually quite verbal; beyond the embodiment of a character, it rarely depends much on physicality. The interview, usually, is the precursor to a scene between the two actors, which is indeed what we got with the gladiator greeting; we just got it full of physicality.

Physicality is using the body and movement to express a character's age, self-image, confidence (or lack thereof), emotions, thoughts, objectives, actions, etc. It supports the improvised spoken words as well as how characters interact and relate to situations in each improvised scene.

Many people are already comfortable with the physical demands of improv. Before even attempting to speak in a scene, they move and mime; I explore this in one of the exercises below. One student, Paula, loved to dance, moving with grace and power. She was always my go-to for physicality-based games. However, to build that dialogue muscle, she worked hard and continuously. A good, physical game offers leadership opportunities for the Paulas of the world and builds confidence to move into other areas of performance.

Here is a list of four areas of physicality to work on with improvisors to build finesse.

Physicality and Guiding Questions

Area of Physicality: **Facial Expressions**

Q: How do you show different emotions with your facial features?

Q: Where do your eyes look when talking to someone? Do they look directly at the person or look away? Why?

Area of Physicality: **Gestures**

Q: How do you use your arms? Why?

Q: Are your gestures close to your body or extended? Why?

Q: What do you do with your hands when on stage? Do you fidget, or are you a master of tranquility?

Area of Physicality: **Stationary and Locomotor Movement**

Q: How do you use your body to express character, objectives, emotion, thought, action, etc. in stationary positions as well as through movement?

Q: When you stand still, do you keep your limbs close to your body, or do you hold them in another position (e.g., bent, supported, extended)?

Q: How do you move from one place to another?

Q: What is your speed? Why is that important to think about?

Q: If you walk, are you a slider, a stomper, a tiptoer, etc.? What does that say about the character you are playing?

Q: If you use adaptive devices (e.g., wheelchair, braces) to move from one place to another, how do they inform or affect your characterization when you move around a space?

Area of Physicality: **Levels**

Q: How do you use high, medium, and low levels to express character and emotion?

Q: How do you use levels to show certain activities?

Q: How do you use levels to show your character's level of power or status?

Diagram #4: Physicality and Guiding Questions

SKILL-BUILDER WORKSHOP GAMES/EXERCISES

GAME TITLE: *Move On*

DESCRIPTION: Group members move as they are able through a space while a controller calls out different emotions, states of being, or other suggestions that shape the movement.

LEVEL: Beginner and upward

GROUPING: Whole group

NOTE: Some people refer to this game as "Walk On," but dubbing the game is not inclusive of those who move differently. Tip of the hat to my friend Jaehn Clare, a self-proclaimed mermaid, for raising awareness of this.

INSTRUCTIONS:
1. Define the movement space and explain that participants are to use the space and move in different directions, not around and around as if on a track or at a roller-skating rink. They should change directions as it suits their wants during the game, being cautious of other movers and considerate of sharing the space.
2. Explain that this game is SILENT. No words, no sounds, no sound effects. Silent.
3. Have participants move around the room in their normal style and ask them to be aware of their bodies as they travel. Where are their hands? What specific movements (if any) do they do with

their feet? Their hands? How is their posture? Where do they look when they move around the room?

4. Call, "Freeze!" and give them an emotion (e.g., nervous, rushed, joyous, giggly), a character (e.g., a rushing executive, a friendly clown, Hamlet, Scarlett O'Hara), an animal (e.g., penguin, giraffe, yak, otter), or some other descriptor that influences the way they move around the room. Cue them to move and later freeze the movement to give a new directive.

Coaching Suggestions:

- Encourage them to make the movements bigger than life—large-scale.
- Ask: Are you looking at others or avoiding eye contact? See what happens when you do the opposite.
- Reinforce the concept of silence.
- Tell participants to be aware of the part of their body that seems to lead them forward, the part of their body that is out in front.

Modifications:

- Tell movers you will shout out different parts of their bodies to lead their movement. You might have them lead with their foreheads, bellies, right shoulders, noses, etc.
- If suggesting animals, consider adding the suffix "-like" to each animal, such as "elephant-like" or "kangaroo-like." Encourage them to remain a

human character with movements influenced by animals.

- Have movers add a silent acknowledgement as they pass others in the space.

Debriefing Questions:

- Were you familiar with the game before playing? How did you feel about playing it again or for the first time?
- How did this game help you explore physical movements?
- What other skills do you think this game builds?
- If you played the leading-body-part version, discuss different characters that might lead with that body part. Explain your answer.
- How will this game help the troupe create better improvisation scenes?
- How can you apply this game to everyday life?

GAME TITLE: *Team Mirror, Paired Mirror, Three-way Mirror*

DESCRIPTION: One or more people do the same movements of a leader, as if they are the mirror image of that person.

LEVEL: Beginner and upward

GROUPING: Pairs; leader with one whole group; leader with two groups

INSTRUCTIONS:

Team Mirror
1. Have all participants stand as they are able and face the leader.
2. The leader slowly moves, and all participants mirror the leader's movements.
3. Remind mirroring participants to remain in their own spaces and not interfere with other participants' activity.

Paired Mirror
1. Pair participants, facing each other, and designate the first leader in each pair.
2. Leader moves slowly, and the follower mirrors the movements. Strive for precision.
3. Call out, "Switch leader!" and have the partner take over leading the exercise.
4. Repeat several times.

Three-way Mirror
1. Select a leader to stand—visible to the rest of the group.
2. Have the rest of the group create two lines facing each other, labeled Line 1 and Line 2. Using one-to-one correspondence, make sure each member as a partner to watch.
3. The leader takes a position facing Line 1; therefore, the members of Line 2 have their backs to the leader.
4. Line 1 members will focus on and follow the movements of the leader; Line 2 members will

focus on their partners in Line 1 and follow their movements. Line 2 never turns around to look at the leader.

5. After a designated time, either have the leader change positions to face Line 2, or have the line members switch places so that Line 1 members have their backs to the leader. Repeat the process.

Coaching Suggestions:

- In the team and three-way versions, the leader should be easy to see.
- To make movements simpler to follow, encourage leaders to keep their head facing the group.
- In all three, have leaders use levels (high, medium, low).
- In "Team Mirror," encourage the leader to create a story and pantomime slowly for others to follow.
- During "Paired Mirror," cue leaders to use locomotor movement to travel around the space. Remind them to move slowly enough for their partner to mirror the movement with precision.
- Coach leaders to explore their own physical movement, using some movements of their partners when it is their turn to lead again.
- In "Three-way Mirror," remind the line members with their backs to the leader to stay turned away and focus on their partner. It's tempting to look at the leader, but line members are building skills that will help them in improvisational scene work.

Modifications:

- Play music to influence the tempo of movements. This is helpful for "Team Mirror."
- Have everyone do the paired exercise and exchange leadership, back and forth, without cues. Let the leadership flow from the movement.
- Have the leader pantomime a story for their partner or group to mirror. For example, a pantomime might be waking up and getting ready for an event such as an Olympic event, a dance recital, or a baseball game.

Debriefing Questions:

- In addition to exploring physical movements, what skills do you think each version of "Mirrors" teaches?
- Which version was more challenging? Why?
- How did the different versions help you expand your own ideas of movements to use as a leader?
- Which role did you enjoy most: leader or follower? What does that say about you as an improvisor?
- Do you think the Three-way exercise is one that multiple teams can practice simultaneously? Why or why not?
- How will this game help us create better improvisation scenes?
- How can you apply this game to everyday life?

GAME TITLE: *Sculpture*

DESCRIPTION: Participants mold each other into character statues.

LEVEL: Beginner and upward

GROUPING: Pairs within full group

PREPARATION: Before playing this game, determine whether you want students to touch each other to "mold" the clay. If your students can do this appropriately, explain that they must touch the person slowly and respectfully with open palms.

If you believe it would be best for them NOT to touch each other, use the "command the clay" mode or "mirror me" mode.

Command-the-clay mode: The sculptor tells the clay what to do.

Mirror-me mode: The sculptor models the exact position for the clay to take, and the clay mirrors and holds the position.

INSTRUCTIONS:
1. In pairs, determine who is Person A and who is B.
2. A will be the sculptor. B will be the clay. Then they switch roles. Clay cannot do anything to itself; the sculptor must mold, command, or model for the clay (see the Preparation note above). However, this clay, upon a request from the sculptor, has

been imbued with the ability to stand, sit, or lie down.

3. Assign the sculptors a theme and have each artist sculpt the clay to reflect a stationary interpretation of it. Encourage sculptors to create body positions that reflect the energy of the theme; make sure they include facial expressions. The clay should be able to hold the positions for quite a while if keeping its feet on the ground or being supplied with chairs or other props.

4. When the sculptures are ready, have sculptors step away and observe the various interpretations by the group. Give the sculptors the opportunity to adjust one or two things in their creation's position, then step back again to observe.

5. Tell the sculptures to relax, switch roles with their sculptors, and repeat the process.

Coaching Suggestions:

-   Depending on the mode used for creating the sculptures, make sure sculptors communicate clearly with clay. Encourage them to be very specific with words and movements.
-   If artists/sculptors have a brain freeze and cannot think of anything to do with the clay, tell them to put their clay's appendages into a variety of positions.
-   Encourage sculptors to think how curved, straight, bent, and twisted positions convey movement and intention of the sculpture itself.
-   Remind them that this is an exercise in communicating creativity. Lead well and follow well.

Modifications:

- Assemble groups of three, and have one sculptor mold two lumps of human clay. Encourage creating a visual that expresses a relationship.
- When the sculptors gather to review their statues, offer them the opportunity to change one minor detail on another artist's statue and then discuss how the change modified the artist's original intent. This might require you to assign one sculptor per statue.
- Give the clay the power to make a sound. Either let the artist assign a sound or let the statue itself interpret its position to create a sound.
- Have the sculptor give a repetitive movement to one portion of the sculpture. The movement should reinforce the original intent of the pose.

Debriefing Questions:

- How did this game use the four areas of physicality? Reminder: facial expression, gestures, stationary and locomotive movement, levels.
- Which was more challenging, being the artist/ sculptor or the clay? Why?
- When you were the sculptor, how did you plan your work of art? What did you do first? Second? Last?
- When you were the clay, what did you want to say to or ask your artist?
- How did each sculpture—in a stationary position—express movement?
- How will this game help us create better improvisation scenes?
- How can you apply this game to everyday life?

GAME TITLE: *Space Rebound*

DESCRIPTION: Actors create two-person tableaux that blossom into scenes upon cue.

LEVEL: Beginner and upward

GROUPING: Pairs within the whole group

INSTRUCTIONS:
1. In pairs, have partners select Person A and Person B. Remind players this is a silent game unless or until cued to speak (see Modifications).
2. The facilitator (you) calls, "Move!" At that cue, both partners use the power of their bodies to move, both in place and around the space, until the facilitator calls, "Freeze!" On that command, partners freeze, holding whatever position their movements landed their bodies in.
3. The facilitator calls, "Person A, step out." Person A unfreezes and steps to the side to observe Person B's frozen position.
4. The facilitator calls, "Go!" Person A interprets Person B's position, then steps back into the scene in a different pose, creating a brand-new relationship, scene, or tableau that "rebounds" off Person B's frozen pose
5. When Person A has taken a pose, A says, "Go!" Person B unfreezes, stepping out of the scene to study it with the intent to create a new scene or tableau that "rebounds" off Person A's frozen position. When ready, Person B steps back into the scene with a new pose that relates to Person

A's frozen position, thus creating a new scenic tableau, and says, "Go!"

6. Continue this process several times, with the partners cueing each other to "Go!" when ready.

Coaching Suggestions

- Coach partners to make large movements and big poses, stretching their bodies to the limit, using levels, and moving in unusual ways. The bigger the moves and positions, the more you give your partner to work with—the easier it is to create a new picture.

- Ask questions to help the rebounding person decide what the new scene is: What is this person doing? What is this person looking at? What is happening around this person? Where might we be?

- Partners may pose close to each other or far away, as long as they create a position that relates to their partner's pose.

- Remind partners not to start a Space Rebound scene with a question. The scene initiator should give information, both physical and/or verbal—off of which their partner can rebound.

Modifications

- With intermediate or advanced students, the facilitator calls, "Freeze and observe!" Partners take three to five seconds to observe each other's positions. The facilitator calls "Space Rebound," the cue for the partners to begin a scene based on their positions. Allow at least three exchanges of dialogue between actors before calling "Freeze!" and showing which person, A or B, should step out to continue creating their tableaux.

Debriefing Questions
- What did you notice about the game as we continued each rebound?
- What challenged you in this game? Why?
- How did you use your Improv Listen skills?
- What did you learn from your partner in this exercise?
- How is this game about reacting?
- What are the pros and cons of reacting skills in everyday life? What will you need to do to discern the difference?

ACKNOWLEDGMENTS

First and foremost, thank you to every improv student I've had the honor to work with and learn from. You continue to inspire me, and it is a genuine pleasure to continue to know many of you as adults who still make me laugh from the back of the house. You know who you are, and you know I love you.

Thank you to my team of theatre-teacher readers: Josh, Chris, and Grady. You provided me with excellent guidance, called out forced metaphors, challenged me to conjure better material, and made superb suggestions. You volunteered your time, talent, and energy, and I am eternally grateful.

Thank you to the teachers of improv—Josh, Heather, and Joe—who lent their expertise and offered their own stories for me to ponder. You are the heart and soul and funny bone of educational theatre.

Thank you to my fellow improvisors and leaders of Laughing Matters and Now This! who shaped me as a performer and educator. Tommy, you breathe life into these pages and will always be one of my favorite improv husbands. Carol, you said "Yes" at a time when I needed it most. To my other improv husbands and sisters, you are forever in my head. That's mostly a good thing.

Thank you, Ashley, for pushing me to clarify EVERYTHING. You somehow took my mishmash of ideas and made them sparkle.

Thank you to the folks at SPS, especially Ellaine, for steering me on the pathway to make this book come to fruition.

Thank you to my editor, Margaret Harrell, who managed to make me feel good about my work while finding opportunities to improve and polish the words, phrases, instructions, etc. Each brushstroke identifies you as a master wordsmith.

Thank you to my girls, Katie and Abby, and the fur babies, Oolie (RIP) and Maybelline. You make life worth living.

Most of all, thank you to my husband, my partner in life, Paul. You are patience personified, sitting beside me on the roller coaster days, structuring my scattered ideas, and making me a better writer and person. You are and always will be my joy and comfort and MRFL.

NOTES

ABOUT THE AUTHOR

Nancy L. Meyer has made up stuff her whole life. She's been a teacher, education director, instructional STEAM (science, technology, engineering, arts, and math) coach, arts integration specialist, innovative teaching and learning manager, trainer, copy editor, writer, professional improvisational comedy performer and coach, professional jazz vocalist, artistic director, musical theatre performer, wife to Paul, and—most importantly—mom to Katie and Abby.

Your review makes a difference!

Need a question to spark your review? Try one of these!

Which parts of this book interested you? Why?

Did you recognize someone you know
in one or more of the stories?

What did you find enlightening/entertaining/practical?

How will you use the information in the book?

Please head over to Amazon to leave an **honest** review.

Thank you very much,

Nancy

Made in the USA
Middletown, DE
25 September 2023

39343597R10106